CORPORATE STREETFIGHTER

·CORPORATE· ·STREETFIGHTER·

HOW TO EXCEL IN BUSINESS AND LIFE USING BRAINS, CUNNING, AND FINESSE

DR. JEFFREY LITWIN

Forbes | Books

Published by Forbes Books, Charleston, South Carolina.
Member of Advantage Media.

Forbes Books is a registered trademark, and the Forbes Books colophon is a trademark of Forbes Media, LLC.

Printed in the United States of America.

10 9 8 7 6 5 4 3 2 1

ISBN: 979-8-88750-048-5 (Hardcover)
ISBN: 979-8-88750-090-4 (Paperback)
ISBN: 979-8-88750-049-2 (eBook)

LCCN: 2022916047

Cover design by Matthew Morse.
Layout design by Analisa Smith.

This custom publication is intended to provide accurate information and the opinions of the author in regard to the subject matter covered. It is sold with the understanding that the publisher, Forbes Books, is not engaged in rendering legal, financial, or professional services of any kind. If legal advice or other expert assistance is required, the reader is advised to seek the services of a competent professional.

Since 1917, Forbes has remained steadfast in its mission to serve as the defining voice of entrepreneurial capitalism. Forbes Books, launched in 2016 through a partnership with Advantage Media, furthers that aim by helping business and thought leaders bring their stories, passion, and knowledge to the forefront in custom books. Opinions expressed by Forbes Books authors are their own. To be considered for publication, please visit **books.Forbes.com**.

*Dedicated to my wife, Donna; my children, Maya,
Jacqueline, and Benjamin; my mother, Rita; my brother,
Adam; and my late father, Meyer.*

CONTENTS

PREFACE

COMING OUT FOR THE BELL

Growing up in Brooklyn and being the youngest and smallest person on my block of row homes, I was frequently the neighborhood punching bag. Maybe I was hit too many times in the head (that would explain a lot); nevertheless, I never backed down from a fight, even though I rarely won. But I did hate to lose. Never showing fear despite the odds at least made it clear that I would land a few blows before the fight was over, and that in itself was somewhat of a deterrent and a minor victory.

When a new kid moved onto my block who was a year younger than I but four inches taller and twenty pounds heavier, my "friends" encouraged him to fight me to show how strong he was. Well, he was in for a surprise, as even though he was bigger and stronger, I won that fight. His mother called my mother to say that I was a bully for picking on her son and that it wasn't right, as he was new to the neighborhood. My mother asked her to bring her son outside and said she would do the same. Well, after one look at my size, his mom said, "I can't believe that he beat you up," and I learned that although

I would never be the biggest or the strongest, I could tough things out and win the day.

When not dealing with the physical aspects of growing up on my block, I would take respite by playing chess with my more intellectual friends and some adults. I was a pretty good chess player in my youth, and what I could not do physically I could often accomplish psychologically by beating my opponents at chess. Chess is a great strategy game, as one learns to think several moves ahead and learns that there is always an opportunity to turn the tables and win the game, even at the last moment. Importantly, I studied my opponent and played against what I saw to be their weaknesses rather than sticking to one strategy. In my younger years, most of my opponents had great memories and played the moves they had learned from books. It was hard for me to compete with that, so I quickly took the games off book and made it a battle of strategic thinking where I had an advantage and often won.

As I approached my teen years, the physical fighting stopped, but the mental fighting continued. Psychiatry was my best subject in medical school, and it really comes in handy in the corporate world. Whether you are dealing with your bosses, peers, or the people who work for you, using psychology is important in reaching the desired result. Everyone is different and is motivated by different things; it is important to learn what motivates each individual in order to be successful. There is a bit of finesse required here, and not everyone can excel at this, but you will find that if you pay careful attention to the people in your circle, you will develop insights that will prove invaluable. Describing to people what I do as a coach, I say, "Think of me as a business psychologist." My job is to help you find your way to a successful career.

My own path to success is not one that I would recommend, as it involved very little planning, many disappointments, and a lot of intuition and opportunism. At the age of five, I decided I wanted to be a doctor. As my parents never went to college and no one in my family had ever gotten a professional degree, I guess I would have to say that this was a "calling."

At the age of fourteen, I got my working papers and began my road to the medical profession by volunteering at Coney Island Hospital in Brooklyn, New York. All new volunteers started as ward clerks, whose job it was to enter temperatures and blood pressures into a graph on the patient charts. The volunteer office was on a floor that had male diabetes patients, several of whom had one or both legs amputated.

As we were walking by these patients, I saw the mutilated limbs with scars and skin flaps, and no one was wearing a prosthesis. I began to get nauseous, and I remember thinking, "Please, God, put me on any floor but this one!" You guessed it; they told me that I was just to stay put and work on this floor. I thought that this would signal the end of my medical career before it started and that my prayers weren't answered. But perhaps they were, as the patients on the ward would come and chat with me often, and I stopped seeing them as amputees and started seeing them as a bunch of great guys who happened to have lost their legs. My medical career was not over yet.

After two years at Coney Island Hospital, I had the opportunity to work in a kidney transplant research lab at Downstate Medical Center in Brooklyn. I was to interview with Dr. Samuel Kountz, the head of the department of surgery and a world-renowned kidney transplant surgeon. I was told that he was the youngest chief of surgery in the hospital's history and the first African American to hold that role at Downstate.

My interview was scheduled for 1:30 p.m., but at two o'clock we were notified that Dr. Kountz was still in surgery and that they did not know when he would be done. I was asked if I wanted to reschedule, but as I was already at the hospital, I said I would wait. I waited and waited, and at four thirty, the person in the volunteer office was getting ready to leave, so she called the department of surgery and was told that the surgery had finished thirty minutes earlier, but they assumed I had gone home.

I was escorted upstairs to meet with Dr. Kountz, who greeted me with a warm smile, and we had a nice conversation. The opportunity to work and do research with such a prominent physician was very exciting, and when the interview was done, I asked him when I would learn if I got the job. He told me I had the job when I walked in because the fact that I sat and waited for him for three hours told him everything he had to know about me. This taught me a lesson about persistence that I never forgot. I worked in the transplant lab for two years and left determined to become a kidney transplant surgeon under Dr. Kountz's tutelage.

Dr. Kountz was a great man, a great surgeon, a compassionate physician, and an innovator who had pioneered many new techniques in transplantation. He traveled all over the world teaching transplantation techniques but unfortunately caught a debilitating disease while traveling in South Africa. The disease left him bedridden and unable to communicate, and he passed away only a few years later at a young age. I had no interest in going back to Downstate if he wasn't there. I had managed to get into medical school to complete my training. I then decided that I would pursue a residency in internal medicine instead of surgery.

I completed my residency and decided to do a fellowship in cardiology. Upon completing my training, I went out in the world just hoping to take care of people and to be of service. Unfortunately, I learned that the real world was not like the academic world I had come from. Cost containment seemed to be more important to many people than actual patient care, and access to medication was more limited than I realized.

On my first day in practice, I received an angry call from a patient who was at the pharmacy to get the medicine I had prescribed. He said, "Do you have any idea how much this medicine costs?" I told him that I honestly had no idea, as no one teaches that in medical school or training programs. But when he told me the price, I was shocked. I then worked with the pharmacist to find something less expensive.

One day I was seeing a patient of mine who was unresponsive to the cardiac medications I had put him on. I told him he needed a cardiac catheterization and perhaps bypass surgery, but he refused to consider it. I told him to see another doctor, as I liked him and could not stand to watch him die, but he said he wanted to keep me as his doctor. In frustration I asked, "Are you even taking the medications I prescribed for you?" The patient looked at his wife and then looked back at me and said he was. I then asked why he looked at his wife when I asked the question and told him that I thought he was not being honest with me.

The patient swore that he answered my question truthfully. I then asked, "Are you taking the medications exactly as I have prescribed them?" It was a question that set the tone for much of how I specifically addressed issues in the future. He then came forward and told me that he had been taking medicine A on Mondays, medicine B on Tuesdays, and medicine C on Wednesdays and that he repeated that for all three medications. I realized that he did not have a therapeutic dose of any of them, and that was why he was still having chest pain.

I went to the sample closet and gave him the medications he needed, and he did extremely well after that.

After that I became friendly with all of the pharmaceutical company sales representatives who came to my office and stocked my closets with huge amounts of medication to supplement what my patients could not afford. And an amazing thing happened: keeping my patients compliant with their medication increased their health dramatically, and very few needed to be admitted to a hospital. I decided to investigate working in the pharmaceutical industry and eventually went to work for Wyeth-Ayerst, a large pharmaceutical company.

TRAINING CAMP

At Wyeth I worked in the medical affairs department, which gave me a lot of exposure to medical marketing. I enjoyed the creativity of the marketing and sales group, and it expanded my thought process, which had been totally science based up to that point. My boss felt that I had strong organizational skills that I had no awareness of, and he gave me several projects that I performed successfully. Unfortunately, he was not an advocate of taking a creative approach to the job, and he was quite comfortable with the slow-moving culture of the company. I realized that it would be difficult to continue to improve my knowledge of business in this environment, and then a headhunter called, and I went to work at Nutri/System.

Nutri/System was everything that Wyeth was not—fast moving, highly creative, and brimming with energy. My title was deputy medical director, and I was to have responsibility for several departments including health research, the call center, convention exhibiting, and production and delivery of nutrition materials to our centers. Nutri/System was my equivalent of getting an MBA, as I learned about timelines to production and how call centers work, trained myself on computer algorithms, and most importantly learned how businesses run. They started me off by putting me in "boot camp" where I did every line job in the company from bagging food to nutritional and behavioral counseling to running a center and selling radio time. At the time I did not appreciate the value of this, but once I made it to the home office, I realized I now had an understanding of what people in the field did that was invaluable in doing my job. In all of my executive jobs since Nutri/System, I have had my new executives go through a boot camp prior to starting their "day job," as without a boot camp they will generally get busy doing what they were hired to do without ever really learning the business.

Nutri/System was the best, most proficient sales organization I had ever seen both at the corporate and the site levels. They invested heavily in the training of employees, and while there, I became a businessperson who happened to be a doctor versus a doctor trying to function in the business world. Unfortunately, the corporate division of Nutri/System declared bankruptcy due to overinvesting and bad timing. I still remember sitting there thinking, "What have I done? I am a doctor, and I am unemployed. I never thought this could happen."

After Nutri/System I knew the kind of work that excited me, and I tried to find a position that would need my newly acquired skill set. I had many job interviews, and recruiters were getting upset with me for trying to expand upon the jobs that were available in an industry that left little room for creativity. I really did not want to settle, as enjoying my work was important to me. I decided that I was a "left-handed widget," a doctor who liked operations and marketing in a world where no one thought a doctor could, or should, have either of those jobs. But on the other hand, if someone ever needed a left-handed widget, I was confident that I would be their guy!

A company named ERT was looking for a left-handed widget, and a recruiter who used to work at Nutri/System told them that they knew the only doctor who would fit the bill. I got an interview with the CEO and chairman of the company, and when we were done, he told me that I would be "bored out of my mind" working for his company but that I should be president of another company he worked with in New York City, a global physical exam company called EHE, and that he was going to call the owners and tell them so.

The owners of that company already had someone in mind for president, so I joined the company as their chief operating officer. When I started, I certainly was making positive changes, but I now realize how much I did not know. I learned everything the hard way, but you do not forget when you learn things the hard way. After six weeks on the job, one of the owners called me in and told me that I was obviously bright and hardworking, but she was disappointed that I had not transformed the business. I was shocked and told her that I felt lucky to understand the business after only six weeks. Over the next several years, I was able to increase the quality and profitability of EHE while continuing to hone my skills as a leader and a businessperson.

BECOMING A CONTENDER

Seven years later, the chairman of ERT reached out to me and said that he was surprised how well I had done at EHE, as he didn't think that anyone could have made that company profitable. He called to invite me to lunch, as he had an opportunity that he felt I would be interested in. After sarcastically thanking him for putting me into a situation that he thought had little chance of success, I agreed to meet him and the company's new CEO for lunch.

At lunch I was offered a job for half of my salary, a bonus that would get me to two-thirds of my salary, and a bunch of stock options. My response was to put my wallet on the table, and I told them to just take that as well. I told them that the stock would have to at least double for me to be kept whole, and the chairman responded, "If it doesn't, it will be your fault. That is why we want to hire you!" I laughed, but it was probably the best answer for someone like me.

I had always thought that the chairman of ERT was a creative genius but a horrible implementer. I was sure that my implementation skills would be an excellent complement to his creative skills and that we might be able to do something together that was both creative and fun. In my first six weeks with the company, I found items that were not billed for, a vendor that was not delivering, inefficiencies in the operations, and discounting of services that were hurting the bottom line. This added up to about fifty cents per share in additional earnings and good positive movement in the stock price. Did I rejoice in this? *No!* Instead, I reflected on the conversation I had with the owner of EHE and lamented that she was right: you can change a company in just six weeks. I shared this with my wife, who asked what was different about me now compared with then. My only thought was, "I am seven years smarter and more experienced." Interestingly, it also occurred to me that had I not left EHE, I wouldn't have known how much I had grown.

During my time at ERT, I ran global operations, I did a stint as head of sales, I ran our consulting business, and I eventually became the CEO of a public company. I had always thought that, having been a COO several times, the step up to CEO would be a small one. I was wrong! The pressure and loneliness in that job is far greater than in any other position. The toughest part is knowing that you are responsible for the livelihood of many people and that their families are depending on you not to screw it up.

There were many things that I wanted to do at ERT, but the board was risk averse. Eventually, a private equity company agreed to take ERT private. In my first eighteen months as CEO, I had grown the company, come up with a new strategy, made that strategy happen by working with a private equity firm to buy us as well as to purchase another business for our growth, and presented to bankers to raise capital for the acquisition. That was one hell of a learning curve in a very short period. Less than four years later, the company was sold for a very good return on investment.

GOING FOR THE CHAMPIONSHIP BELT

After leaving ERT, I started a consulting business so I could work with whom I wanted to when I wanted to. I also partnered with a former colleague to start an eConsent business, as I had never done a start-up before, and I thought it would be both interesting and fun. As part of my consulting business, I was asked to evaluate a potential acquisition for a company called WCG. The CEO invited me to lunch, and after a short while, we were completing each other's sentences on how a business should run. I was asked to join the company, and I said no; I was done with corporate jobs and liked working for myself. I told him I would be happy to consult for WCG, but I wasn't going to give up the lifestyle I had.

It seems that I have been continually drawn to companies with three-letter names! Five meetings later I had met the executive team, liked the company's mission, and convinced my wife not to divorce me if I took another corporate job. The CEO said that he wanted me to be his partner, the COO of the company. I was unsure if I was ready to go back to work at all, so I asked him to give me the most difficult job in the company. At the time, it was integrating two companies that they recently acquired that had formerly been competitors. When I took over, the companies were well behind their plan, and there was a lot of work to be done in all aspects of the business. Eight months later we were well ahead of plan, operations had improved dramatically, we had built a strong management team, and we had created significant shareholder value. I am convinced that this was the best work I had ever done, and it was gratifying to see the culmination of what I had learned throughout my career.

I then took the position of COO and spent a lot of my time mentoring others. The good work of all of those at WCG led to a successful sale, and for the first time since I was five years old, I was sure of what I wanted to do. I wanted to coach people and give them the benefit of the school of hard knocks that I had attended for the last thirty years.

The difficulty I had initially in the corporate world drove me to invent a new way to fight for what I wanted to achieve. Moving up the corporate ladder to CEO and creating considerable value for all the stakeholders of the companies I led can be traced back to the rough and tumble of street brawling coupled with the intellectual maneuvering of chess and the insights of psychiatry. This, combined with the hard-learned lessons of managing corporations, is what I call *corporate street fighting*.

In the world today, you have to fight for what you want and what you believe in. By sharing my experiences and insights, my goal is to enable you to excel in business no matter what business you are in. Whether you are a corporate executive or an entrepreneur, as a corporate streetfighter, you will be able to reach ever greater heights in your business and personal life through brains, cunning, and finesse.

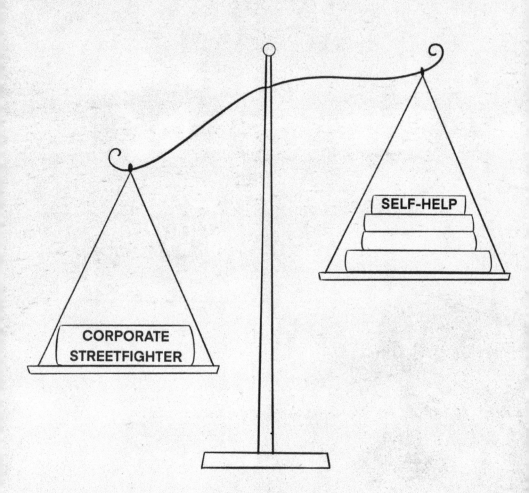

INTRODUCTION

WHY SHOULD YOU READ THIS BOOK?

Jeff's true superpower is his ability to work with extremely difficult people, keep a smile on his face, and get things done those others cannot. He has been successful while working for some of the most difficult people I have known and does it all while advocating for his direct reports and treating them with respect.

—CORPORATE EXECUTIVE AND BUSINESS FOUNDER

Corporate street fighting is all about learning and applying the strategy to go the distance. Let's start with the obvious question—why should you read this book? Here's the reason. This book will show you exactly how to work with your boss, whether you are in your first management position or one step away from becoming a CEO, whether your boss likes you or wants to destroy you. Corporate street fighting is about knowing the ropes and being able to take the heat. Will you be able to fight for what you want to achieve, or will you have to throw in the towel because you didn't take the time to understand what really was going on in the ring? This book will give you the tools to go the distance and win the fight of your career and of your life.

Have you ever felt that you were suffocating at work? Have you known the feeling that either your boss or the work itself has you in a choke hold that is squeezing the life out of you? Have you found yourself just gasping for a little more breathing room and trying to find the right jiujitsu move to free you up long enough to get things back on track? Well, you are not alone.

I have had that feeling, and many of the people I have coached along the way have as well. This book will help show you the way to free yourself from these situations, and more importantly, you will learn how to avoid putting yourself in this position. Yes, you heard me right; you probably put yourself in that position, and you don't even know it!

Two people can be given the exact same task and reach the exact same result but be judged differently based on how they present their work to their boss.

Two people can be given the exact same task and reach the exact same result but be judged differently based on how they present their work to their boss. In this book, you're going to find out why. The person who is judged harshly will chalk it up to the boss not liking them or that the other employee is one of the boss's favorites. This "Woe is me" approach allows the employee to blame their failure to be recognized on circumstances out of their control. To be a true corporate streetfighter, you need to understand that you are in control, and you can change things for the better.

The sooner you become a conditioned and skillful streetfighter, your instincts will become second nature, and you will work your way up the ranks to become a leading contender for career advancement. You will learn that working smarter is better than working harder and that becoming a corporate streetfighter will bring you greater success while providing you with more time to spend with family and friends.

BECOMING A CORPORATE STREETFIGHTER

You will need to master two core components to become a corporate streetfighter. For that reason this book is divided into two chapters, one on *how to manage your boss* and the other on *how to manage yourself*.

Managing Your Boss

The first core component is *taking control of your relationship with your boss*. A great deal of work-related stress is related to the pressure your boss puts on you. When you learn how to manage your boss, you will decrease the stress you experience. You can direct much more of what happens at work and decrease the anxiety caused by unrealistic or unmet expectations. You will be in the driver's seat of your career and your future and not just hanging on the ropes, trying to regain consciousness from the latest onslaught.

This book will not teach you how to change your boss

Anyone who is married or has been in a long-term relationship can tell you that starting a relationship with the hope of changing someone is generally not going to turn out well.

because there is little chance of that happening. It's about *managing* your boss and managing the situations you find yourself in with your boss. Anyone who is married or has been in a long-term relationship can tell you that starting a relationship with the hope of changing someone is generally not going to turn out well. This is even truer with your boss. At least your significant other loves you and therefore has a reason to try to change. But in the workplace, your boss does *not* love you and has little motivation to change their behavior.

After all, there is a reason that they are the boss and you are not. They have earned their way to a leadership position by delivering for the business either as an individual contributor or by the output of the departments they lead. Neither of these things necessarily makes them a person who is easy to work for. Their personality is already set, and they already have an opinion of you and your capabilities. If you are lucky, very lucky, your boss is a mentor who is invested in your career. If you do not have such a boss or are just lost in a large organization, you need to find a way to break through, get noticed, have your work and ideas recognized at a higher level, get promoted, and most importantly make more money and have a better life. Reading this book and applying what you learn will put you on the path to becoming a corporate streetfighter and achieving your goals.

Faced with the choice between changing one's mind and proving there is no need to do so, almost everyone gets busy on the proof.

—JOHN KENNETH GALBRAITH

Managing Yourself

The other core component is how you manage yourself. I am going to address what you need to do to take control of your career. Since you can't change your boss's behavior, the only thing you can be sure of changing is *your own behavior*. That's where the strategist in you will be important. Corporate streetfighters are not "yes" people, brown-nosers, or kiss-assers to the boss. This book will teach you how to win by being true to yourself and your beliefs. Often, just a bit more preparation or a minor spin in how *you* present things can be the difference between getting what you want and being dejected after having an idea ignored or being passed over for a promotion.

As you study the Corporate Streetfighter Method, you will learn what is expected of you in different corporate positions, how to get promotions and raises, and how to avoid behaviors that are hampering your advancement and having a negative impact on your personal life as well.

As a senior executive, I have helped many aspiring executives become corporate streetfighters. Today I continue to work as a coach and mentor helping senior and junior executives, fast-tracking entrepreneurs, and successful family business owners and heirs to become corporate streetfighters.

Coaching and mentoring are my passions. I firmly believe that everyone can benefit from coaching. You may say, "I am really good at what I do. I don't need a coach." But even if you

This book will be most helpful to those who are good at what they do but not receiving the recognition they deserve.

are great at what you do, coaching can make you just a little bit better. And being even a little bit better can translate into an exponential difference in your success.

The world's greatest athletes all have coaches, and they are the best in the world. The same is true for singers; they sing better than their coaches, but they can still learn from them. This book will be most helpful to those who are good at what they do but not receiving the recognition they deserve. Is that you? All of us should continue to learn throughout our lives. We will never be the best we can be if we stand still, while progress marches on.

The coaching method I use is to share stories from my own career both as an employee and as a business leader and highlight the lessons learned that transformed me into a corporate streetfighter. I have been blessed with a couple of mentors, but mostly, my bosses have been difficult to work with (OK, a few would best be characterized as a bit crazy or, because they were well to do, eccentric), and I have had many obstacles to overcome. I have written this book to share these lessons with you so you can avoid some of the painful experiences I have encountered and have a more fruitful career and life. If you follow these instructions and implement them well, you will excel at what you do and become a *true corporate streetfighter*.

WHY LISTEN TO ME?

There is no magic to becoming a corporate streetfighter. It's about *strategy and tactics*. The ideas I am going to share will be eye-openers as to why things have worked or not worked for you in the past. By following the Corporate Streetfighter Method, you will learn the reasons why some of the things you've done have worked, why others have not, and how to go about increasing your odds of success in the future.

You will learn many new things in this book, but you will also find yourself saying, "I knew that." I will teach you how to add new tactics to your armamentarium and also to what you know and haven't acted

Doing the right thing is not enough to excel. Doing the right thing consistently is.

upon yet to achieve a better career, a better relationship with your boss at work, and a better life in general.

Ready to enter the ring? Good, then read on.

Here's the first lesson: Doing the right thing is not enough to excel. Doing the right thing consistently is.

As a corporate streetfighter, you manage your bosses, and you manage your career with focus and consistency. By doing *what works* again and again as opposed to now and again, you'll get the results you are looking for. A good fighter trains and spars well in advance of the big fight so they are prepared when they enter the ring when it counts. I call the lessons "rounds" in keeping with the theme of this book—that of fighting your way to the top of your game as a corporate streetfighter. As you read on, take some time after each round to think about the lessons and how you can apply them. As you do your job, work hard not to lose sight of what you learned and apply the lessons immediately and confidently so the constant distractions we all have to deal with will not derail you from your long-term goals and ultimate success.

I started in business as a complete novice, and it is no secret that most doctors make poor businesspeople. Fortunately, with my history of street fights, playing chess, interest in psychiatry, intense competitive nature, and desire to win, it turned out that I had a certain knack for business that I did not recognize in myself. Luckily, there were others who recognized my potential and who put me in situations where I could increase my knowledge and experience. I also had a few mentors who brought me to realizations that I would not have reached on my own. In several of those cases, I only came to understand what I had learned years after the lesson was taught. As I advanced through the business ranks, I found that mentoring others and sharing what I had learned along the way brought me both personal and professional satisfaction. I wrote this book to continue in that pursuit.

> **Perhaps you stay because you love the company, even though your boss makes you miserable, or perhaps you stay because you just don't have the energy to leave.**

Unfortunately for me but fortunately for you, I have had a lot more bad bosses than good ones. Bad bosses have you losing sleep on Sunday night, knowing that another week of work is ahead the next day, and you have no idea how many bombs they will drop and, more importantly, how many will land on you. These are the times you likely feel powerless. You need the job to support yourself or your family, and you feel trapped. Perhaps you stay because you love the company, even though your boss makes you miserable, or perhaps you stay because you just don't have the energy to leave. In any event this book will give you the solutions to make the best of these situations and to turn them around so that you have more control of your career and life.

By recounting conversations and stories that were part of my career experiences, I endeavor to give you a sense of the thought process the parties had at the time. Sometimes it only takes one spark to change your thinking, and that can lead to tremendous changes in your professional and personal lives. In these pages you'll find that spark and see that it benefits you as well.

In one of my companies, we had a product that was relatively new to the market. It was a good product, and we were gaining market share, but we were also having some issues and not growing as quickly as we would have liked. I heavily pursued and then bought the company of a competitor that was the number two provider of these services. I was asked to justify this acquisition, and my response was that they had been around for twelve years, and I was buying their history of mistakes and the knowledge they gained from them. In reading this book, you are buying my history of mistakes, the self-reflection that took place, the knowledge I accumulated, and the experience that was garnered. All of these factors have led to a successful career and to my great passion to share this knowledge and experience with all of you.

You will note that I use quotations liberally and that many of them are from Theodore Roosevelt. Spoiler alert: He was my childhood hero and certainly was a man who got things done and ignored many of the obstacles in his way. To my mind that is to be admired. Why so many quotes? Because so much has been said over the years in a manner that cannot be stated better by me, so why not "delegate" to those who have already said it best?

I rarely meet a person who does not want more money or career advancement. But in most cases, when questioned, they have no idea how to go about achieving either of these goals. Often, they feel that they are more deserving of these rewards than their superiors do and are confident that they are more qualified than their peers. Most people feel that a promotion should be expected every couple of years if they put in a good day's work and do a reasonably good job. In some places that is the case, but it is not the best way to run a business. In general, communication between bosses and employees is poor, expectations are unmet on both sides, and often both the employee and the boss feel misunderstood. The employee feels undervalued, and the boss often feels that productivity is not what it should be.

The most surefire way to ensure that you are heard, recognized, and appreciated is to *change the way you approach your work and your boss.*

Although there are definitely issues with both bosses and employees, I have chosen to focus this book on the employee's perspective. *Why?* I have learned that it can be hard and, at times, impossible to change the way your boss works and thinks (perhaps their boss can have some impact on that), so the most surefire way to ensure that you are heard, recognized, and appreciated is to *change the way you approach your work and your boss*. How do you do this?

I am not suggesting that you become a "yes" person to incur favor with your boss in order to get promoted. Instead, I want to encourage you to approach your job, career, and relationship with your boss in a different manner to increase the likelihood that you will achieve your own career goals. You must learn to master the ways of the corporate streetfighter.

I know this is not easy. I always considered myself a good boss, and I was generally described as "tough but fair" by those who worked for me. However, most of the bosses I had encountered were not very good managers or communicators.

I polled some of my coworkers and learned that they had as many bad bosses as good ones. It got me thinking, "Why do the higher-ups keep promoting these people into important jobs?" The answer seemed to be that the executives really did not pay much attention to how people managed their subordinates as long as the work got done. At the same time, they did reward people who they felt were loyal, kept them informed, and helped them achieve their goals and objectives.

Executives don't seem to care if credit is taken for other people's work, only that the work was creditworthy. How many times in your career has your boss's boss asked what your contribution was to a project or what you did to contribute to a successful client experience? Probably never. Your boss's boss may have no idea what your contribution is and is not likely to find out from your boss! Only the best of bosses is going to sing your praises or talk about your contributions to his/her boss. Is that your boss? If it is, consider yourself lucky! This was not something I had ever really thought of, but understanding this dynamic resulted in a fundamental change in the way I approached my job and the way I communicated in the future.

A DIRTY DOZEN OF EXPERIENCES WITH MY BOSSES

Below are just a few quotes from some of my bosses and my boards of directors to give you an idea of what I have had to deal with in my career.

- Why do you insist on trying to do something to make a difference? Can't you just sit at your desk, take longer lunches, and reap the benefits of annual increases and more stock options?

- Although the project was a huge success, I told you not to do it. You put me at risk by doing it, so although I got a promotion and a bonus, I am giving you nothing to teach you a lesson.

- I believe that you have to break a person down completely and then rebuild them to make them better.

- I embarrass people in public because when I was publicly embarrassed, I learned something and never did it again. These people keep doing the same thing over and over again despite being embarrassed. Why are they upset? They should be learning.

- You are the only person who has worked for any of our companies and has survived being in our doghouse. Everyone else either quit or got fired.

- Don't bother coming to the next board meeting if you have the same results as this quarter. Just send a resignation letter.

- We have interviewed over thirty external candidates and have decided you are the best candidate for the CEO position, but we don't think you will be better than the prior CEO, so we are offering you a lot less money to do the job.

- I know we agreed to financial terms in our last meeting, but in reviewing the contract, we noticed it is what we told you and agreed to but not what we meant, so we are decreasing our offer.

- We are a team, and we must respect each other in front of the staff, so in every meeting, you must agree with me whether you agree with me or not. If you disagree, you can approach me in private.

- I am completely open to an exchange of ideas. During this meeting we will exchange your ideas for mine.

- As you know I believe that all decisions must be logical. Your logic is faulty, and mine is not. So I will tell you what is logical and what you need to do.

- We want to thank the management team for increasing the value of this company thirtyfold. We did not feel it appropriate to reward you with a bonus or additional stock, so we are presenting you with this plaque instead.

And the most common of all boss behavior is just yelling with no purpose at all, so there isn't even something worth quoting. Please visit my website at www.corporatestreetfighter.com and feel free to share some quotes from your bosses. And check out my weekly podcast, where I give advice on how to deal with your boss.

AN UNFORGETTABLE LUNCH

Perhaps the all-time topper was not a quote but an action. It was our vice president of sales's fiftieth birthday, and the boss took him out to lunch. We were all waiting for them to come back to the office for a surprise party and were happy that the boss took him out of the office so we could prepare.

Two hours later we were all waiting to spring the surprise when I saw the sales VP waiting by the elevator with a box in his hand. I ran out to bring him into the room we were waiting in to surprise him when he told me the boss just fired him. First, I laughed, as it was so ridiculous, but then I realized it was true. I asked him to talk to me before he left and brought him to the room where everyone yelled surprise. He expressed that it was a bittersweet moment for him because he just got fired. Again, no one believed him at first, but then everyone got the message. To top it off, the boss, seeing the party was on, decided to come and hang out with the team as if nothing had happened. Writing about it now so many years later, it still seems that no one could be that indifferent and clueless, but it really did happen.

How I dealt with these bosses varied based on where I was in my career and in my life. Early on I spoke my mind to a point, but I was early in my career, house poor, and with a family to support, so there were times I pulled my punches. As I became more business savvy and had more of these experiences, I became more confident and hardened to tough comments, and things that might have brought a tear to my eye in the past now just made me *mad*. And I fought for what I wanted to do or thought I deserved.

In the following chapters and rounds, I present many different examples of the behaviors and actions of my bosses, along with my responses and the specific strategies on how to steer through these rough encounters and navigate your way to career advancement. If you use these lessons, you're on your way to becoming a skilled and knowledgeable corporate streetfighter.

CHAPTER 1:

MANAGING YOUR BOSS

WHAT KIND OF BOSS DO YOU HAVE?

I may not always be right, but I am never wrong.

—MAJOR LEAGUE UMPIRE

Bosses run the gamut from great on one end of the spectrum to %?$#&* on the other end. A good place to start is determining where on the spectrum your boss fits. By taking the following brief questionnaire, you can quickly get a more precise feel of what kind of boss you have.

QUESTION	Y	N
My boss always thinks he/she is right.		
My boss is a micromanager.		
My boss takes credit for my work in front of his superiors.		

QUESTION	Y	N
My boss blames me or members of their team when things go wrong.		
My boss publicly embarrasses people.		
My boss frequently loses his/her temper.		
My boss wants to mold everyone in his/her image.		
My boss plays favorites in hiring and promotions.		
My boss likes to personally "save the day" on all major problems.		
My boss uses intimidation and fear to drive productivity.		
My boss is very self-centered and egotistical.		
My boss spends more time managing up than managing their subordinates.		
My boss talks about people behind their backs.		
My boss only gives me feedback at the time of my review.		
My boss doesn't listen to my ideas.		
My boss wants to mold everyone in their view of perfection.		
My boss sets unreasonable deadlines.		
My boss does not understand that I have a life outside of the office.		
My boss rarely discusses my career development with me.		
My boss makes many promises but rarely keeps them.		

Now for each answer of yes, give yourself one point. Add up the total number of points to get your boss's score and see how your boss stacks up.

If you get a score of three or less, you are in good shape. After all no one is perfect. Reading this book may give you some good ideas and can help you plot your career strategy, but you are in good hands.

If you get a score of four to six, your boss has several characteristics that are troublesome, and this book will help you better understand your boss and your approach to your current job and your career.

If you get a score of seven to ten, you have found the right book. Your boss is difficult to deal with, and you need to apply what you learn from this book to see if that can make your day-to-day job and your life easier and less stressful.

If your score is eleven or higher, let me start by saying I am sorry. You are in a very difficult situation, and a job change might be something you want to seriously consider. Reading this book should help you make the best of it, changing things from extremely difficult to something more tolerable, and perhaps most importantly, if you do change jobs, you can start your next job on the right foot and avoid some of the situations that make your current job so difficult.

CORPORATE STREETFIGHTER STRATEGY—ASSESS THE LANDSCAPE AND APPLY THE TACTICS

In order to move forward in your lives and careers, you need to understand best practices (i.e., lessons learned) and make them a part of your thinking and actions. At the end of each, I provide the lessons that can accelerate your success.

Lesson 1: Take Stock of Your Current Situation

The questionnaire above is a means to put some data behind any feelings or emotions you may have in regard to your boss. In all situations, by knowing where you are, you can take the best course of action to get where you want to be.

Lesson 2: Use the Information, Insights, and Especially the Lessons I Provide for You to Guide You to the Best Possible Responses to the Situation You Are In

Use this better understanding of your boss to your advantage. By making the lessons your own, you will get the results you're looking for. This way you can tackle the problems with your boss with the confidence of a corporate streetfighter.

ROUND 2

REALIZING THE POWER OF MANAGING YOUR BOSS

The executive team was in the boardroom meeting with the company president. We were nearly done with the meeting when his administrative assistant entered the room to tell him that the owners of the company were on the phone. He excused himself, and the CFO lamented that he had three important questions to ask the president, and he hoped he would return soon.

I said, "Ask me the questions, and I will tell you exactly what the president will say." He laughed, but I insisted that I was not joking and that I was confident that I would give him the precise responses that he would get from our leader.

The first question was a simple one about financing a new project, and I told him that the president would say that he was not prepared to finance that project at this time. When the CFO asked why, I told him that the president would tell him that it was his decision at this time and that he did not want to discuss it further. The CFO said that was not really an acceptable response. I agreed and told him that it was not my response, but I was confident that it would be the response he would receive.

The second question had to do with how to handle certain expenses in regard to whether they should be operating costs or capital expenditures with depreciation schedules and, if so, over how many years. I told the CFO that the president would get a bit belligerent, as this was not a subject in his wheelhouse and would tell him that he is the CFO and that he should be the most knowledgeable about these matters and that instead of asking him these questions, the CFO should be making a strong recommendation for the president to determine whether or not he agreed or disagreed.

The final question was a complicated one that I did not think the president would be able to answer. I told the CFO that he would not admit that he could not answer the question and would not want the rest of the team to know, so he would just up the ante on the belligerence incurred on the prior question and tell him that he was wasting the team's time by asking it in this forum and that they should follow up privately. I was sure that the president would look at this question as a means to embarrass him in front of the group.

Several minutes later the president returned to the room, and the CFO said that he had some pressing issues to present. The president asked him to proceed, so the CFO asked the first question. The president's response was exactly as I predicted, and there was some laughter in the room. As the president had simply said no to a request, he did not understand the levity and asked why people were laughing. The CFO said he would tell him shortly and asked to proceed. The second question was asked and answered just as I predicted, with the president's belligerence increased by the laughter. The president again demanded to know why everyone in the room was laughing, and the CFO said he would tell him after the final question was addressed. You can guess what happened; the answers were all precisely as I had predicted, almost to the word.

The whole room was now laughing uncontrollably, and the president was furious. The CFO finally revealed the answer to the president's question about the laughter. "Jeff could be you," he said. "He knew exactly how you would answer every one of the questions, and he told us so while you were out of the room."

The president never realized that I had engineered my way back into good standing by studying him so intently that I could predict his reaction in almost any situation. Thankfully, because his ego would not allow for the fact that someone he felt had nowhere near his intelligence could do such a thing and since none of my peers specifically "outed me," he never really connected the dots.

THE RIGHT MOMENT

Improving my standing was great, but I still wanted to get several things done, and my boss was pretty much against anything I suggested. Most doctors are consultative, and they enjoy the back-and-forth of an interesting discussion. This is what I was used to.

The president did not function this way. I learned that if you brought something up and he said no, he would not allow that subject to be brought up again. Therefore, I realized that I could not bounce any ideas off him. If I had an idea that I wanted to pursue, I had to succeed the first time out of the box, which meant I had to be completely prepared before having any discussion with the boss. After that I never asked for anything without having all the ammunition I needed in advance. And I started getting results at a high rate that was noticeable to my peers.

I also watched the boss's mood carefully, as there were times that the best argument would not win if he was in a bad mood. I learned to wait for another day when I was more likely to be successful.

Unknowingly, I had developed what was likely the most important skill for my career growth. As the Boy Scout motto says, "Always be prepared." Developing the skill of excellent preparation with just the right amount of information, without extraneous data, helped me get what I needed for the rest of my working life.

DETERMINING THE BEST WAY FORWARD

Why did I start with this story? Because just a few months earlier, I would come to work every day waiting for the ax to fall. In general, I enjoyed my work, and I felt I was making a good contribution to the company; however, I was the victim of constant verbal abuse from the president, and he had undercut my credibility with the owners of the company who originally hired me.

Of course, when I asked my boss why the owners had turned on me, he denied saying anything to them and stated that he did not know what had changed their minds about me. Certainly, the easiest thing to do would have been to find a new job and resign, but I put together a plan that proved to change the entire trajectory of my career. I have outlined my thought process in the following chart:

ALTERNATIVES	ACTIONS	ACCEPTED/ REJECTED
Alternative 1	Go to the owners and complain about the boss.	Rejected
Alternative 2	Ask my boss for permission to ask the owners why they decided that my work was now unsatisfactory.	Accepted
Alternative 3	Call the owners but make the conversation totally about my performance.	Accepted
Alternative 4	Try to get my boss to understand my position and change his behavior.	Rejected
Alternative 5	Change my behavior and my approach to my boss.	Accepted
Alternative 6	Test different approaches to see what works.	Rejected

Alternative 1: Go to the owners and complain about the boss—*rejected.* Aside from the fact that I find going behind the boss's back to complain distasteful, it is highly unlikely to be successful. The owners have placed the president/CEO in that job for a reason, and they are much more likely to side with the CEO and view you as an uncooperative problem. Others had quit the company and complained to human resources on the way out the door, and the owners had stayed with the CEO. So why should my complaining, especially since he had already discredited me with them, do any good at all? They would likely be happy to have me leave.

Alternative 2: Ask my boss for permission to ask the owners why they decided my work was now unsatisfactory—*accepted.* It occurred to me that by telling me he had no idea why the owners had turned on me (they wouldn't even speak to me when they saw me), he had opened the door to me asking to speak to them directly to clear the air. After all they hired me before they hired him, and they were pleased with my work until he arrived.

Alternative 3: Call the owners but make the conversation totally about my performance—*accepted*. I called the owners, and they made it clear that prior to hiring the new president, we had a plan of action that I had not fulfilled. They were correct, as the new president changed my priorities when he came on board. I shared this with them, and they were skeptical. So I was very direct—I asked them what I needed to do or show them that would make them see that I was capable of delivering. They told me explicitly what they would need to see, and I assured them that I would deliver on this within three months (see more on the evolution of this in round 5).

Alternative 4: Try to get my boss to understand my position and change his behavior—*rejected*. There was little chance that my boss would change his behavior. He thought he was right in all things, he had the confidence of the owners, and I was an excellent scapegoat for him (which was probably the reason I still had a job).

Alternative 5: Change my behavior and my approach to my boss—*accepted*. As it was extremely unlikely that my boss would change his behavior, it became clear to me that I had to change my approach to working with him. While doing so, I had to take a long, hard look in the mirror and reflect on how I was interacting with him and why I was failing in his eyes. I realized that I was still operating as I had when I reported to the owners in regard to my approach to the work and my collaborative communication style. However, my boss did not like collaboration; if you went to him with an idea and he said no, you could never bring it up again. I had to come up with a whole new approach.

Alternative 6: Test different approaches to see what works—*rejected.* Considering the precariousness of my position, feeling my termination could be imminent, I didn't think I had many opportunities to get this right, and if I kept coming to my boss with new angles, he would probably feel badgered and become dismissive or angry.

Considering all six of these approaches, I decided to carefully think through a new approach and not try it until it was well formulated. I recognized I had one shot to get this right, and I could tweak some things as I went along if it was working. Psychiatry was one of my best subjects at medical school, so I decided to use those skills to study my boss's behavior and come up with a plan to succeed. And that is just what I did.

MY ANALYSIS OF MY BOSS'S BEHAVIOR

- **Mood and demeanor:** My boss was a moody guy. I watched this carefully each morning and could tell what his good days and his bad days were. I decided that no matter how urgent the situation was, there was no point in approaching him on a bad day, as he would not be in the mood to engage.

- **Analysis:** I watched his behavior in every meeting. What types of answers put a smile on his face? What made him angry? What conversations kept him in his comfort zone, and which did not? I studied how he responded to certain types of questions. I knew I had to package anything I presented to him to conform with what I had learned.

- **Preparation:** Excellent preparation is extremely important. It has helped me throughout my career, and it will do the same for you. As my boss did not like collaborative discussions, I felt the only way to get what I wanted or needed was to get all the possible data I could prior to meeting with him, be prepared for any of his questions, and score a quick win without giving him the opportunity to find fault, as the preparation was so complete. I never went into his office to ask for anything that I could not defend to the hilt. By watching him I was able to anticipate most of his questions, but generally with excellent preparation, you will be ready for any question. I started "winning" all the time. My peers were amazed at the change in the boss when it came to dealing with me. And until the opening dialogue at the beginning of the round, they had no idea how I had been doing it.

CORPORATE STREETFIGHTER STRATEGY—ALWAYS BE PREPARED TO DEFEND YOUR POSITION WELL

What does this story tell us?

Lesson 1: As a Corporate Streetfighter You Should Always Be Prepared and Play to Win

The more questions your boss has to ask, the less confident they will be in your suggestions.

Do not waste your boss's time with poorly thought-out ideas. Take the time to prepare a comprehensive plan that is hard to ignore. Very often the more questions your boss has to ask, the less confident they will be in your suggestions. Anticipate their questions to the best of your ability and always have the answers already in your presentation.

Lesson 2: Do Not Try to Change Your Boss

The odds of you changing your boss are extremely low. Still, you can take control by modifying your own behavior to fit the situation and to get the result you desire.

Lesson 3: Learn What Gets Your Boss's Attention and What Does Not

We are all in a lot of meetings. Do not just pay attention to your own presentations. Watch others present as well. See what the boss responds well to and what goes poorly and adjust your presentations accordingly.

ROUND 3

HOW THE WORST BOSS FORCED ME TO DEVELOP THE SKILLS FOR SUCCESS

The person hired as president of a company I worked at was the subject of round 4. This was also the same person responsible for the firing of the sales VP in round 2. He was tall and good-looking, came from a wealthy family, and had degrees in multiple areas from several Ivy League schools. The owners of the company were very appearance conscious, and they could not have found a leader who kept up appearances better. But he was a poor boss and had few leadership abilities.

As a fellow physician, I suffered the most under his leadership because, unlike finance and sales, medicine was a subject he knew well and one that he could have his most prolific arguments about. I was constantly a target of abuse, even though I and my peers felt I was doing a good job. He bad-mouthed my work to the owners, and they would literally ignore me when they saw me, even though we had had a good relationship prior to the hiring of the president.

The day after my first child was born, one of my employees called me at home and told me I had better not take the rest of the week off. She said it would be best if I returned to the office tomorrow as the president of the company had spent several hours snooping around my desk and speaking to my employees, and she was fearful he was trying to get me fired.

For my part I had previously decided that since I had spent less than three years at each of my first two jobs, I should try to put in at least five years at this job so my résumé did not have the appearance of someone who could not see things through. (Yes, I know no one cares about this anymore, but back in the old days, people did care about things like this!)

How to survive in this hostile environment was a mystery to me. I was sure I was doing a good job but could not convince the owners of this. Then the president said he wanted to decrease my responsibilities and hire someone new to take those responsibilities on. This was clearly the first step in my ousting.

He did say that he would have the management team vote on any candidates he suggested and that if they did not want to hire someone, he would take it under advisement. My colleagues rallied around me and said that they would not vote to bring someone new in. I told them to please vote to bring in the new person, as I was confident that any new person, especially a physician, would find the job unbearable, and that would only serve to strengthen my position. If the new person was able to succeed with even half of my responsibilities, I was willing to concede that perhaps the president was right and that I was not delivering. In any event getting fired would be a relief at that point, as I could not continue to stay in such an abusive environment.

With some of my responsibilities taken off my shoulders, I had the time to think about the position I was in and what to do about it. This was not something I had done in the past. What would I have to do to get the owners to see that I was doing a good job? How could I get my boss to agree to allow me to do the things I needed to be successful? If I did these things, could I make my job bearable or even enjoyable once again?

As stated in round 4, I asked his permission to speak directly to the owners, and he surprised me by agreeing. When I asked, "What do you need to see from me in order to start moving our relationship back in the right direction?" the owners proceeded to tell me what they would like to see and when they would like to see it. This was a major breakthrough for me, as I now had a goal that I knew I could deliver on.

What I did not understand was I thought I had already been delivering on this goal, but they did not. Why not? My job was to transform our international physician provider network. In my time with the company, I had taken the overall satisfaction ratings from 20 percent excellent, 65 percent good, 10 percent fair, and 5 percent poor to 55 percent excellent and 40 percent good and 5 percent fair, so clearly, I had been doing something right.

I also produced a monthly report that showed the gross changes I was making in the network. The owner was unimpressed and said that the total network size was only changing by a few providers each week, and that was unacceptably slow. I took this to heart and realized that, based upon the information I was providing, that would seem to be the case. But with my newly discovered "You can only change yourself, not your boss" philosophy, I decided to repurpose my report and show everything my team and I were doing, showing every doctor who was let go and every doctor who was hired.

The report was impressive and showed that although the gross numbers were barely moving, we were removing about forty physician facilities a month and replacing them with much higher-quality sites. The report was very well received, so I backtracked to show the total changes over the last six months.

This was a lot of work, and many would claim it was not necessary, but I had found the "secret sauce" to regain the trust of ownership, and I wanted to cement my path back to good standing. This worked so well that I overheard a conversation between the owners and the president where they asked him directly, "How could Jeff be such a bad employee if he is doing such good work?" The answer from my boss was, "When we limit the things he does, he can do good work." This was incorrect, as it was all in the presentation, but with a new employee handling a portion of my old job, I was able to both have a life and be respected at work.

The boss never gave me a hard time again, and when the physician hired to take over part of my workload quit (as I expected), I did not ask to get those responsibilities back again, as I was not power hungry, and I did not want the boss to feel that I was going to be competitive with him. Besides, my personal life had improved dramatically, allowing me more time to spend with my family. I needed time to destress after the ordeal I had gone through.

CORPORATE STREETFIGHTER STRATEGY— IMPROVE THE WAY YOUR WORK IS PRESENTED

A famous chess player once said, "No one ever won a chess game by resigning!" No matter how difficult the situation appears, there still may be an opportunity to win if you look hard enough.

Lesson 1: It Is Not Enough to Know You Are Doing a Good Job If Your Boss Does Not Agree

You have to present what you are doing in a manner that allows for that work to be recognized. Bosses are not psychic (see round 4). They only know what they are told or shown. It may feel like a lot of extra work just to improve the way your work is presented, as the job should speak for itself, but time and again, I have seen missed opportunities due to the lack of diligence in this area.

Lesson 2: Think Carefully about the Purpose of Your Work Rather Than Just Doing Your Work

I had done a good job but had not connected the dots in my presentation to what was important to those in charge. Just presenting the work without connecting it to the mission is never enough.

Lesson 3: Learning Is a Lifelong Pursuit

Even the most difficult of bosses has something to teach you if you can separate your emotions from the interaction. In some cases you will see traits that you want to emulate; in others you will see traits that you want to avoid. But always continue to learn, and you will become a black belt in corporate street fighting.

YOUR BOSS IS NOT OMNIPRESENT OR PSYCHIC

When I ran operations, I made it a habit to meet with my direct reports on a weekly basis to review their metrics, discuss items that needed to be addressed, help them prioritize projects, and do some mentoring. These meetings were an open forum; I would generally ask any questions to follow up on things I needed to know, and then the employee could ask to discuss anything that was on their mind.

One of my best employees used this opportunity to tell me how fed up he was, despite the fact that we had a good relationship, because I had given him no support on a recent project. He said that he had spent the last five weekends in the office working, and I had not even acknowledged his efforts. Instead, he argued that all I did was continue to press him for timelines on projects that were not getting done. The conversation went something like this:

> **ME:** Do you think that I have a video camera in your office that records your time in the office and what you are doing?

EMPLOYEE: No.

ME: Aside from the times that I seem to know, by your nervous state in our meetings, when you have not done your metrics, do you think that I am endowed with psychic abilities?

EMPLOYEE: No.

ME: Do you think that I am an omnipresent being?

EMPLOYEE: No.

ME: Do we meet each and every week to discuss your metrics, what you are working on, and your priorities?

EMPLOYEE: Yes.

ME: In any of those meetings during the last five weeks, have you mentioned to me that you need help because you are coming in on weekends and still cannot get this very important project done?

EMPLOYEE: No.

ME: Then why the hell are you mad at me? How am I supposed to know any of this if you do not tell me in the meetings that we have set up specifically for that type of communication?

EMPLOYEE: I just assumed you knew. Now that I think about it, I realize I should have told you.

This circumstance is not as unusual as you would think. Most employees feel that their boss either knows or should know what they are doing or how hard they are working. The reality is most bosses are results driven, which is how they became bosses in the first place. Often, in their minds, how you get to a result is not as important as the result itself. If you really want your boss to understand how you approach your work, then it is up to you to explain it. Even though your boss may never ask, a good boss will use this as an opportunity to do some coaching and to get some insight into your thinking to see if someday you might assume a higher leadership position.

EVALUATIONS GIVE INSIGHT

One of the companies I worked for did a very extensive 360° evaluation where you were rated, and comments were rendered by your peers, your subordinates, and your boss. As I had always seen myself as a strong manager, I was certain my direct reports would speak favorably of me. I was a bit curious as to what my peers thought of me, and I was certain that my boss, who had been very complimentary of my work, would give me a strong review.

This company made a large investment in its employees and this process, and they hired a psychologist to sit and review your 360° with you. I was told two things in this discussion that, although I did not realize it at the time, were to have a major impact on my career. The first was that I needed to be more decisive—more on this in round 23. I was told that, as an executive, my job was to make decisions in a timely fashion and not to wait until all the information was in before making time-sensitive decisions. The second was about how I was dealing with my boss. The psychologist went on to tell me that my employees really enjoyed working for me; they perceived me as being much more supportive than my boss was when he managed them directly. He also said my peers thought that, although I was relatively new, I was bringing value to the organization.

On the other hand, he said the one thing he really needed to review with me was my relationship with my boss, as he saw that to be problematic. I was shocked. My boss had always been complimentary to me and had mentored me in some areas that were quite helpful. He had gotten me one of the biggest percentage salary increases in the company the prior year, and he left me alone to run my divisions as I saw fit.

The psychologist told me that my boss did, indeed, respect my work. My boss said that since I had come to the company, he felt confident in leaving operations in my hands so that he could devote his time to being more strategic and working more closely with the C-suite of the business. This led to the following exchange:

ME: So that matches my thoughts. What is the problem?

PSYCHOLOGIST: When asked how Jeff has taken charge and run things in such a successful matter, your boss had no clue. Don't you ever discuss these things?

ME: I try to bring it up on occasion, but he has no interest. As things are going well, he doesn't feel he needs to be bothered with the details. He leaves me alone to do what I think best, and that relationship has worked well for me, as I enjoy the autonomy.

PSYCHOLOGIST: The problem is he has no idea how or why you are doing anything you are doing.

ME: Why is that a problem as long as we are both happy?

PSYCHOLOGIST: Because when his bosses in the C-suite ask him how you are doing what you are doing, he won't be able to answer them.

ME: Why is that a problem if he tells them how happy he is with me?

PSYCHOLOGIST: Because they will never truly understand your value to the organization.

ME: When I try to talk about what I am doing, he has no interest. He is just happy with the result.

PSYCHOLOGIST: It is your responsibility to make him understand what you are doing.

ME: Why? He is the boss. Shouldn't he be asking if he wants to know?

PSYCHOLOGIST: The point is he doesn't care to know, but it is important for your career that you make him know.

ME: I don't know how I am going to do that.

I had never really thought about all this, but it was true. The owners knew I was doing a good job for my boss, but they had no idea about the extent of my involvement in revamping the way my departments worked or my involvement with other departments within the business. The psychologist had made a significant point; it was important to my career that I make my boss understand what I am doing.

CORPORATE STREETFIGHTER STRATEGY— MAKE SURE YOUR BOSS UNDERSTANDS YOUR CONTRIBUTION TO THE COMPANY'S GROWTH, PERFORMANCE, AND MISSION

I did not consider this to be as big an issue as it really was. As a matter of fact, I pretty much ignored this advice until a later point in my career when I realized how right the psychologist was. As you can tell, I have done a lot of self-reflection in my career and have learned that a lot of the advice I received was good advice, but I just did not appreciate it at the time. And this experience resulted in the following lessons.

Lesson 1: It Is Up to You to Drive the Communications with Your Boss

This is a hard lesson for many executives to learn, especially if you have an unreceptive boss, but it is an essential lesson to become a corporate streetfighter. We all have to practice a bit of psychology at the workplace and figure out the best way to approach our bosses. It is a rare boss who is interested in what you are doing, is complimentary when they should be, and mentors you to advance your career. Therefore, you need to find ways to get the attention needed by driving the conversation. Often this means that you need to change the approach you take, as you should not expect that your boss will change the approach they take.

Lesson 2: When People Take the Time to Mentor You, If the Advice Doesn't Hit Home at the Time, Don't Just Ignore It or Say It Doesn't Apply to You

Even if the advice doesn't resonate with you at the time, file it away for future reference and reflection. Several times I was told things that made no sense to me at the time, and I doubted the applicability and the veracity of what was being said. Several years later something transpired where the light bulb went on, and I saw that I just wasn't ready for the advice I was given, as it was not pertinent to me at that point in my career, but it did turn out to be very good advice.

MY INTRODUCTION TO THE POWER OF KNOWING YOUR BOSS

In the prior round, I reviewed how my boss did not care to know what I did or how I did it, but this same boss was a great mentor in how to manage his bosses. And it was a jaw-dropping lesson for me. Several months after joining this company, it was time for me to present my first large-budget project to the C-suite. My boss told me that I would have about fifteen to twenty minutes for my presentation and that I would probably get my answer immediately but certainly no later than the next day. I was shocked, as I was asking for $5 million, and that process would have taken many months at the company I previously worked for.

A week prior to the meeting, my boss sat me down and said that he wanted to help me with my presentation but that some of the things he would say might be upsetting to me, and he wanted to know if I wanted his assistance. I told him that anything that would help my presentation would be valuable to me and that I was pretty thick-skinned and unconcerned about what comments he might make. He began by telling me that my shoes were awful and that I needed to go out and buy myself some nice wing-tipped shoes with laces. He then proceeded to tell me that my part-polyester, part-cotton shirts were just not appropriate in this business and that I needed to go out and buy myself some nice, new, white, button-down cotton shirts. He even went so far as to say that I should not iron or press them; I should leave the light folds in them so people can see it was straight from the box! He then went to my ties, which (what a surprise) he hated. None of them were full silk, and he said that was a necessity to look the part of an executive at this company. After trying to describe to me the type of tie I should buy and where I should buy it, he told me that he did not trust me to get it right and that he would buy the tie for me. Finally, he did tell me that I did have one suit that was acceptable, and that was the one to wear.

None of this upset me, as what did I know about these things? But I was surprised that the conversation was about these secondary items, and we had not yet talked about my presentation. I asked why these items were important, and my boss told me that he knew the audience I would be presenting to and that making these changes would greatly increase my chances of success. As I wanted to be successful, I agreed to do all of the things he suggested.

Then I asked, "What about the presentation itself? Do you want to review it?"

My boss responded, "I trust you completely on the presentation, and I see no need to discuss it or review it." Although flattering, I was taken aback by this, as all of his comments had to do with my appearance and not the value proposition I was presenting. But when in Rome, do as the Romans do.

I took my boss's advice, and the next week, I came to the meeting with the three most senior executives in the company wearing my shiny, new wing-tipped shoes, my white cotton dress shirt straight from the box, my best suit, and the tie he had purchased for me. As the company's leaders were walking into the room, executive no. 1 asked me if I was wearing a new tie, told me he liked it, and asked me where I had purchased it. And as I was about to start the presentation, executive no. 2 commented, "I see you have a new shirt. I used to work for a shirt company. Let me know your size, and I will send you a couple of boxes." All of this really eased my nerves, as I really wanted to make a good impression on my first big presentation.

The presentation went great, and my budget was approved before we left the room. I decided that my boss was a genius! How could he have known? What would have happened if I had dressed differently? Was that as important as the presentation itself? Could it have been *more* important? Was it really all about appearances and little about the substance? Or was it that they trusted me on the substance, but the appearance was necessary for them to view me as one of them? I will never know, but I do know that it certainly didn't hurt to have followed my boss's advice.

CORPORATE STREETFIGHTER STRATEGY— FIGURE OUT WHAT IS IMPORTANT TO YOUR BOSS AND DELIVER ON IT

At the time, I did not connect the dots that this was a great example of knowing your bosses and how to manage up, but it was actually a tour de force example. Getting to know what is important to your boss will pay dividends throughout your career.

Lesson 1: Whether You Like Your Boss or Not, There Is Generally a Reason They Got to Be Where They Are in the Company

Listen to their advice, take criticism well, and then decide whether that advice suits you and your personality. If things go well, take it as a win. If things go badly, take it as a lesson and then reflect upon your performance and whether you executed that advice as well as you could have.

Lesson 2: Often It Is the Little Things That Can Result in Success or Failure

Starting a meeting with everyone in a good mood is much more likely to result in a positive outcome than when people have a negative attitude toward either you or your work. Perhaps if I had come to that meeting with my scruffy old shoes, a polyester tie, a mediocre shirt, and one of my lesser suits, the attendees might not have gotten past that, and much of what I had to say would not have hit the mark.

EXTRA BENEFIT FROM THAT EXPERIENCE

Little did I know that the changes the boss addressed regarding my appearance would pay dividends again. When looking at another opportunity, I interviewed with the CEO of a company in Philadelphia, and he told me that I would be the ideal candidate for a position as president of a healthcare company in NYC. The owners of his company also owned the other company. This was flattering and not what I expected, but a month later, I met with the co-owner of the company for an interview. After the interview, she

Something I deemed to be unimportant might have been the deciding factor in getting my next job.

said that she could see I was intelligent and that she liked the fact that I wore wing-tipped shoes, cotton shirts, and a nice suit but that she had someone else in mind for president and asked if I would consider a COO position. I said I would depending on the compensation, but I must admit that I was a bit bewildered that once again my appearance was such an important part of the interview. If only I could make myself taller! And so it happened again. Something I deemed to be unimportant might have been the deciding factor in getting my next job. And once again, I will never know if I would have gotten the job if I had worn something different to the interview.

Lesson 3: You Never Know All the Benefits of Your Experiences at the Time You Have Them

I joined a company where my appearance was an important part of the corporate culture. It seems that the C-suite executives at that company were not alone in thinking this was important, and it helped me get my next job. In today's world suits and ties are mostly a thing of the past, but you can substitute the folly of wearing a suit and tie in a company where people come to work in jeans and sneakers or any other situation where there is a corporate culture in place where you are seen as being an outsider.

Being part of the culture of a company is generally an expectation if you have managerial aspirations. After all an executive team would be foolish to put someone in charge of a department or division who did not believe in the corporate mission and culture. I encourage corporate streetfighters to fight for what they believe in, but they will be most successful if they can align themselves well within the present culture of the company they work for.

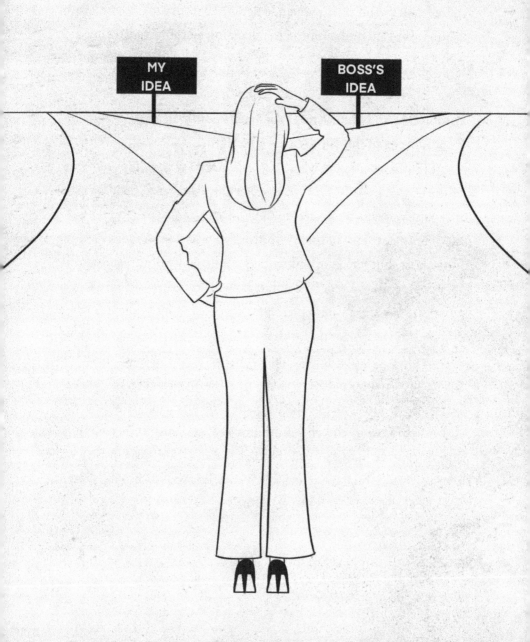

YOUR BOSS NEEDS YOUR SUPPORT TO BE SUCCESSFUL AND VICE VERSA

While traveling to one of the offices of my company, a midlevel executive cornered me to complain about his lack of advancement and that he felt that his boss was ignoring his ideas. He had been passed over for a promotion several times, which he attributed to the fact that he rarely agreed with his boss's approach to the department and voiced his opinion to that effect frequently. He felt he was right about those disagreements, but the boss generally did what he felt best, and that led to this employee being argumentative and often not supportive of the boss's decisions.

I look at conversations like this as teachable moments, and I always ask if the employee has already discussed their concerns with their boss. The employee said he had, but as always the conversation ended badly, with the boss feeling his authority and decision-making were being questioned and the employee feeling that his opinions had not been heard. (Does this sound familiar? It should be as it is quite common.)

I inquired as to whether his feelings were about one particular situation or if it was a chronic problem. After learning the problem was chronic, I asked for specific examples of precisely what transpired in several instances from the employee's point of view. After a few examples, I stopped the employee and told him that, as I noticed a theme, I felt that further examples were not necessary. I asked him to give me the benefit of the doubt, and if I end up missing the mark, he would be free to continue to further elucidate the situation to me.

I had met with this employee a couple of times in the past, and I also knew his boss very well. Both had made me aware of the tension between them, and neither saw a path forward to a productive working relationship. Fortunately, although they disagreed often, neither had questions about the competency of the other. They did disagree on some of the decisions being made and how those decisions were communicated. The conversation went something like this:

ME: When you and your boss have disagreed, have the boss's decisions always turned out badly?

EMPLOYEE: No, some surprised me and turned out well. But that doesn't mean that my ideas would not have been at least as good. And there were other times things had not gone well at all.

ME: When presenting your ideas, are they generally taking into consideration your office alone or all the offices of the company?

EMPLOYEE: My office, but I think that they could work for other offices.

ME: When your boss thinks about these things, do you think he is taking into consideration all offices and the applicability of things across the board or just your office?

EMPLOYEE: I would guess he is looking across the whole company. But as I know my office best, I should be allowed to do what I think is best for my office.

ME: Do you think it wise to have multiple ways of doing things in a company, with each office doing what they want, or one integrated system that works for all offices? Although that might not be a perfect solution for each individual office, it is likely the best solution for the company as a whole.

EMPLOYEE: I see your point, but my ideas are not getting the consideration they deserve.

ME: Can you understand that if your ideas only impact your office and do not address the general needs of the company, your boss would not find your suggestions useful to advance his objectives?

EMPLOYEE: Again, I see your point, but I only want to do what is best for my office.

ME: But we are a company with multiple offices, and we need to work in an integrated manner. Do you support your boss when a decision is made even though it is not what you would have liked?

EMPLOYEE: Honestly, I tend to continue to argue for what I wanted to do, as I believe it would be best.

ME: For your office.

EMPLOYEE: Yes.

ME: But not for the company?

EMPLOYEE: I can't say.

ME: Do you understand that doing the same thing in different ways in multiple different offices, because the employees in that office want to do it their way, would make it difficult for us to operate as one business and would dramatically increase our costs and the difficulty in addressing problems that arise?

EMPLOYEE: Yes, but I still believe I know what is best for my office.

ME: I beg to differ. The office might be *my* office. It is certainly *our* office, but it is not *your* office.

EMPLOYEE: Right.

ME: Who decides whether you get promoted, and who decides what raise you will get at the end of the year?

EMPLOYEE: Obviously, my boss.

ME: Do you think your boss is more likely to reward those who help him achieve his corporate objectives or those who argue with him and distract him once a decision is made?

EMPLOYEE: I see your point, but …

ME: If your ideas do not benefit the corporation as a whole, can you understand why they are not accepted? If you want to advance in the company, you need to think globally as well as locally. If you present ideas that represent the whole company and support and assist your boss in achieving his objectives, you can achieve your personal objectives. Instead of hoping your boss will promote you or significantly increase your compensation, you will earn that recognition and compensation. And once a decision is made, you need to support the path selected by your boss 100 percent and give it your A effort without complaint. That is what team players do.

EMPLOYEE: Point taken. Makes a lot of sense. Thanks.

I've seen this play out in every place I have worked. Poor communication results in disharmony and extra work for all involved. Expecting your boss to change is highly unlikely to be productive.

> **Poor communication results in disharmony and extra work for all involved.**

CORPORATE STREETFIGHTER STRATEGY—GET ON BOARD WITH THE COMPANY'S MISSION

The easiest thing and many times the only thing for you to change is your own behavior. Therefore, you should take it upon yourself to try to improve communication and, once a decision is made, to support your boss and aid their success. Those are the people whom a boss is going to want to promote when they move up the corporate ladder themselves.

Lesson 1: You Have to Think about the Company's Goals and How to Adhere to the Company's Agenda

For example, if you work in a company with multiple offices, try to apply what you know about your office to the company as a whole. Corporate is unlikely to proceed with a plan that is different in every office. You need to keep the bigger picture in mind so your recommendations have an impact across the organization and align with what your boss is trying to accomplish.

Lesson 2: If Communication Is Difficult with Your Boss, Try to Figure Out How to Change Your Approach

It's always up to you to make the adjustments. You should never count on the boss changing their approach. Remember, by making your approach work with your boss, you are both adding value to the company and helping your career advance.

Lesson 3: Very Importantly, When a Decision Is Made, Being Subversive and/or Not Giving 100 Percent to the Tasks Assigned to You Will Not Go Unnoticed

It will hurt the company, your department, and your career if, once a decision is made, you fight it. Do your best regardless of what you think of your boss's decisions. The boss has generally gotten that job for a reason, and they may just have something to offer that you haven't thought of.

Lesson 4: One of the Most Important Lessons Is That Failure, to a Degree, Is OK as Long as Lessons Are Learned

I never truly learned anything from getting something right. I might have just been lucky. But when I got something wrong, I reflected on the reasons why and what, if anything, I could have done differently. Those solutions and reflections have stayed with me throughout my career and have become *experience*. A corporate streetfighter should continue to evolve their skills and learn from battles won and battles lost, and some of the best lessons learned are from the battles that are lost.

"But if we do this, everyone will quit!"

ARGUING WITH THE BOSS—WIN WITH FACTS AND KEEP EMOTIONS IN CHECK

Your boss probably believes they are right most of the time, and they have all of the power. Therefore, going to your boss with your opinion of what is better or what you think is right can be an uphill battle. It's often best to sublimate one's ego a bit and go for the win as opposed to fighting to prove you are right.

As I mentioned earlier, I developed the useful habit of getting all my ducks in a row before presenting an argument to my boss, but even with that background, there have been times that I have let emotions get the better of me. Here is an example where the conversation went something like this:

BOSS: I want to close the office in the UK and move it to Cambridge.

ME: That office has been around for years and has done a good job. Why do you want to close it?

BOSS: I visited it for the first time last month, and I don't like the area it is in. It felt unsafe.

ME: We have never had a problem, and no employee has complained. I have been there many times and never had a problem. The area and buildings aren't the best, but it is better than where I grew up in Brooklyn.

BOSS: Well, I don't want to have an office in that area.

ME: There are nicer office parks in the area we can move to.

BOSS: You are not listening. No one has heard of that town, and I want to move to Cambridge, as that is a place where serious companies are located.

ME: I don't think we will be able to keep the majority of our employees if we move to Cambridge.

BOSS: Why not? I hear it is only forty-five minutes away.

ME: Without traffic, but it can take ninety minutes with traffic.

BOSS: Why don't you get me some proof that employees will not move?

I did an employee survey, and a few weeks later, I came back with the results.

ME: I did the employee survey, and we would lose two-thirds of our staff if we moved to Cambridge.

BOSS: What are their biggest issues?

ME: A lot more gas costs, cost of living, and salaries are significantly higher in Cambridge, and the travel time will eat into their personal lives.

BOSS: I want to move to Cambridge. I will increase everyone's salary by 15 percent and give them all a gas allowance. I can't do anything about the travel time.

I went back to the employees again and learned we would still lose half of our employees if we moved to Cambridge. I met with my boss again.

BOSS: So are you going to stop holding up progress and move the office to Cambridge?

ME: We would still lose half of our staff, and if that is the case, we might as well just shut down the UK office.

BOSS: So we will just hire new staff.

ME: Most of the staff have been with us for more than five years and many more than ten. We can't replace their knowledge, experience, and loyalty.

BOSS: I want to move to Cambridge. I am making financial concessions. Now stop complaining and come up with a plan to move and replace the employees who leave. I will not force you to do this. You need to see that I am right and get on board.

This was very emotional for me. I had been to the UK office many times, and I did not want to see half of the staff quit or lose their jobs because of this move. I had done very well in my operating role, and my boss did not want to order me to make this change, as he wanted me to see things his way. But I did not agree with this move, so we were at an impasse.

I had a one-hour drive into the office each morning, and as soon as I would get in my car, my phone would ring, and the boss would spend an hour yelling at me that I was ruining the company by not doing what he asked. This went on for over two months—yes, almost every day for over two months. My subordinates with offices near mine said that I was looking worn out in the morning and worse at the end of the day. My patience seemed thin, and they did not know why, but they wanted the old me back. I was making myself sick over this.

The head of the UK office was also ready to resign if we moved the office. No impassioned plea I had made in regard to the employees had hit the mark, and I was extremely frustrated. One day while speaking to our CFO, I said, "Doesn't the boss realize how much more money it will cost to move to Cambridge?" Then it hit me. I had never made that simple argument, as I was only thinking about the people—something my boss didn't seem to care about. I went home that night and did the math. The office in Cambridge was much more expensive than the nicer offices we had scoped out near the current location. With the car allowances and raises he had already promised and the difference in rent, we were looking at approximately $3 million higher expenses than we had currently, and he had only put $500,000 in the budget for an office upgrade. Making this move would result in a significant hit to our bottom line and would cause our public company to miss earnings.

The next day I was my old self again, using data versus emotion. I walked into the CEO's office, and our conversation continued:

ME: You win. I can't take the daily calls anymore. If you want to be in Cambridge, I will move the office to Cambridge.

BOSS: Finally. I was growing tired of trying to convince you it is the absolute right thing to do.

ME: OK, but I just want to make you aware that it will cost us, at a minimum, an additional $3 million to make the move, and we have not budgeted anything close to that expense.

There was a pause for a minute.

BOSS: Are you crazy? How can you possibly suggest that we move to Cambridge when it will cost that much? We need to stay in the same area we are in today. How much will that cost?

ME: Just a little more than we pay today.

BOSS: Well, get that done ASAP and let the employees know before they all quit.

I wanted to kill him! Seriously, after torturing me and upsetting the entire UK office, now he was not admitting he was wrong and making it sound like it was my idea. That being said, I just swallowed my pride and took the win.

The staff in the UK office were ecstatic, and I felt tremendous relief. It then hit me that I had forgotten to stick to the facts, and I had become too emotional. If I had gone right to the financials, I could have saved myself and everyone else involved a lot of stress and aggravation.

CORPORATE STREETFIGHTER STRATEGY—EXECUTE WELL AND TAKE THE WIN; DON'T GET EMOTIONAL

Sometimes we need to learn a lesson more than once for it to stick. That is very common as long as, eventually, you do learn the lesson. I knew what the right approach was but got distracted by my emotions.

Lesson 1: Keep Your Emotions in Check and Stick to the Facts

We are all human (well, most of us are!), and sometimes we let our emotions get the best of us. You need to be able to recognize when your emotions are taking control and shift back to what is really going to make an impact. It is hard to change your boss's mind, but your best bet to achieve this is with facts and data, not emotions or opinions.

Lesson 2: Don't Give Your Boss an Opportunity to Distract the Discussion

Often when I had my boss on the ropes and was making my point, I would throw in a few more things for the coup de grâce. I have learned that this is a mistake. In sales they say when you have a sale, stop selling. The same is true in discussions; when you are winning, take the win! In the case above, I messed up at the outset by starting with emotion, but had I started correctly and still not won, the reason would have been that I was being emotional, and the boss would have just focused on that issue.

Bosses are great at finding the one thing you say that doesn't truly make your point in a ten-point argument and harping on that to prove they are right and dismiss your other points without remarking on them. Don't give them that opportunity. Corporate streetfighters know how to win, and they take the win when they can get it.

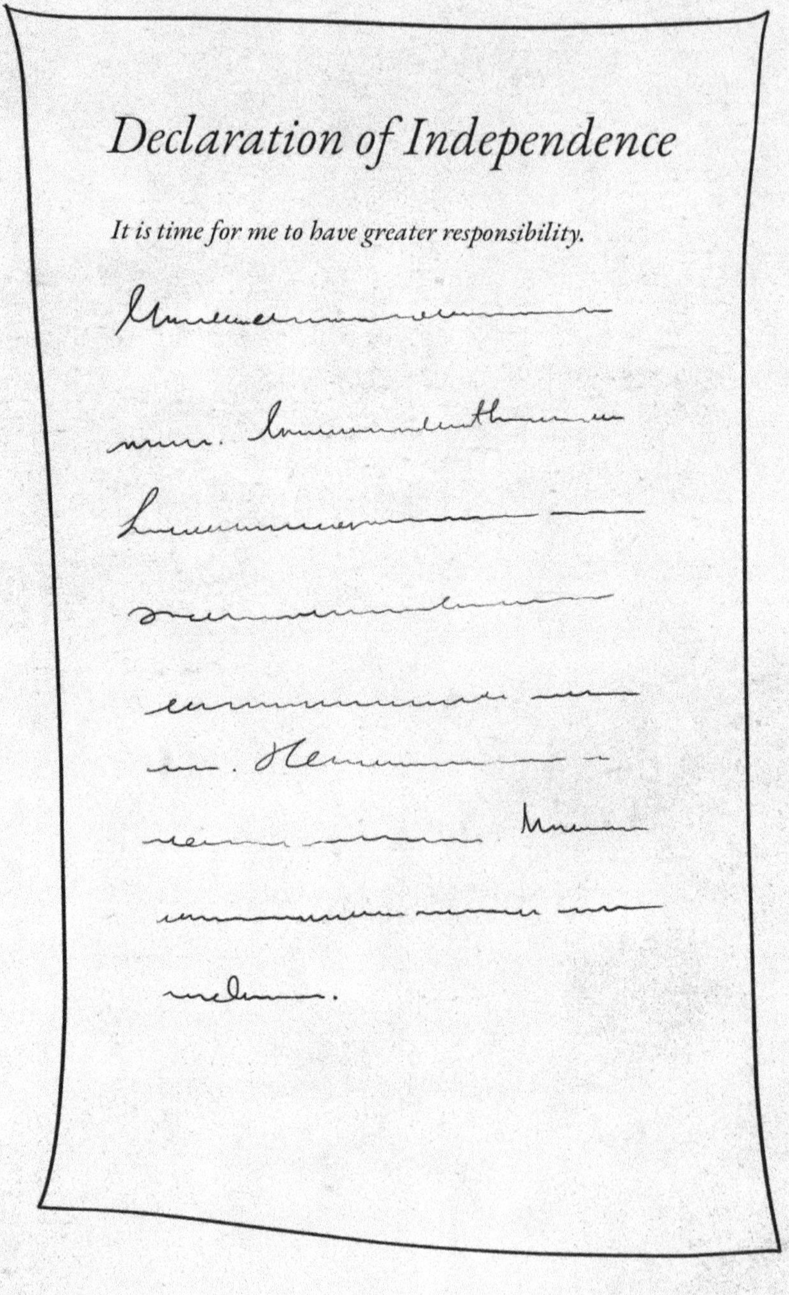
Declaration of Independence
It is time for me to have greater responsibility.

ROUND 8

ASKING YOUR BOSS FOR GREATER INDEPENDENCE

Does your boss think that they are the smartest person in the room? Are they a dictator, a narcissist, an egotist, or none of the above? If so, they may supersede your thinking for their thinking. They may not even give you the opportunity to suggest anything and just *tell* you what to do instead. Of course, your boss may very well be the smartest person in the room, but you will have little to no personal career growth if your path is dictated to you. And your boss will eventually find (if the company grows big enough) that it is impossible to control everything, as they either become a funnel that prevents progress or finally have to depend on people who have not been able to make a decision on their own for years and therefore are probably not going to be able to perform properly.

I once had an executive who had worked for me previously come to me with a concern about his new boss, and we had the following conversation:

EXECUTIVE: I really miss having you as my boss.

ME: Why?

EXECUTIVE: You used to let me make my own decisions, and my current boss just tells me what to do. I don't feel that I am growing personally or businesswise anymore.

ME: Have you expressed your concerns to your boss?

EXECUTIVE: Not in so many words.

ME: Do you disagree with the decisions made by your boss?

EXECUTIVE: Generally not. The thinking is sound, but there are other approaches that would work as well, and I would like to try some of them.

ME: The next time you have an idea that you would like to act on and your boss tells you what to do instead, state how you feel and that you would like to make your own decisions. Say that, as an executive in the company, you feel it is important for you to do so. I bet that will work, but as this seems to be a trust issue, I strongly suggest that you knock it out of the park, so be sure to pick something where you know you will be successful, as this will help build trust.

EXECUTIVE: Thanks. I'll give it a go.

About a month later, I bumped into the executive who came to see me in my office. Our conversation went as follows:

EXECUTIVE: I know what you are going to ask. Did I follow your advice?

ME: Yes, you know me so well.

EXECUTIVE: I did what you suggested.

ME: How did it work out?

EXECUTIVE: Not so well.

ME: I am shocked. Your boss did not let you do what you wanted to do?

EXECUTIVE: No, my boss *did* let me do what I wanted to do, but it was a complicated project, and it did not turn out well, and now my boss is dictating what I should do again.

ME: So you followed my advice on how to do what you wanted to do but ignored my advice to pick a surefire success to start with.

EXECUTIVE: Yes, I'm afraid so.

ME: So you really didn't do what I suggested, and now you are probably worse off than when you first came to me.

EXECUTIVE: I guess I really blew it.

ME: For now, but when you do have a strong opinion in the future, pick something you *know* you will do well on. Then let your boss know that you know you let them down last time but that you learned your lesson and are confident you will get it right this time. Empower your boss by promising to give periodic updates to give comfort that it is going well. Make sure that, the next time, you are able to achieve your goals and earn the boss's trust.

EMPLOYEE: Got it.

CORPORATE STREETFIGHTER STRATEGY—EXECUTE SUCCESSFULLY TO GAIN YOUR BOSS'S TRUST

You may advance your career by following orders from your boss, but when you do advance, you will not be prepared for success. Make every effort to gain your boss's trust and to think for yourself and your department.

> Getting the boss to trust that they can rely on you is a major step in getting further independence and advancing your career.

Lesson 1: Ask to Do More on Your Own, as You Will Learn Very Little Just Doing What Is Dictated to You by Your Boss

If your boss is autocratic in nature, you will need to present a comprehensive plan to show that you have done the thinking and the work necessary for the boss to trust you.

Getting the boss to trust that they can rely on you is a major step in getting further independence and advancing your career.

Lesson 2: Do Not Try to Change the World Right Out of the Box

Do something with a very high probability of success. As you read in the example above, making a great presentation on why you should be able to work independently and then screwing it up may even be worse than not trying! This may require several baby steps before you can take on something larger. Do not get angry if your boss does not let you move quicker—remember, you are trying to get them to a place that they are not comfortable with, and they will be waiting for you to make a mistake to prove their original controlling nature is the correct one. Do not help them by overstretching. Corporate streetfighters know how to pick their battles and win them.

WHEN IS A "GOOD" BOSS ACTUALLY A "BAD" BOSS?

Several times I have inherited teams either by a promotion or an acquisition. On occasion I come across an executive who I have been warned is not up to snuff. I try not to prejudge anyone, but it is not unusual for several of this person's peers to warn me that I should be careful to not let this individual drag me down. My first thought in hearing things like this is, "Why is this person still here if they are so horrible at their job?" And the general answer is that their boss, my predecessor, had been protecting them. Generally, I have been told that the boss likes and cares about this individual and has tolerated the problems with their work for personal reasons.

Sometimes I have found this to be true, but more often than not, my assessment of the individual is that they do a really good job but have made an occasional mistake as we all do. These employees are often very honest and freely tell me about the mistakes they have made and how grateful they were to have the "protection" of their prior boss, and they were wondering if I also would protect them. I have found these situations interesting, as to my mind these individuals were just as good as anyone else on the team and usually much better than the perceptions people had of them. "Why do most people in the company feel this person is unworthy of their position?" I would ask myself. The reason turns out to be that their boss is always making excuses for this person's work, followed by comments that effectively state the employee is worth tolerating because of loyalty or hard work and so forth. I have found that these "protected" employees usually do good work, and they need to be supported but not necessarily defended. In many cases they have impostor syndrome, which is discussed in round 22.

In these situations the boss feels like a good person for protecting the employee, the employee feels great loyalty to the boss for protecting them, and I see a tremendous disservice, as the boss should be owning the work product that comes from their division and their employees and backing up the work produced rather than making excuses under the guise of protecting that person. I have worked hard to restore the reputations of these people when I come across this situation, but it is extremely difficult to undo the damage that has been done. Interestingly, when executives in the company do finally get it and see that the employee is doing an excellent job, they tend to compliment me as the boss for developing them as opposed to giving credit to the employee for having been misjudged in the past.

CORPORATE STREETFIGHTER STRATEGY—DON'T FALL INTO THE TRAP OF BEING "PROTECTED"

Believe in yourself and what you do. Understand the corporate dynamic of what it means to have to be protected by someone.

Lesson 1: Having a Boss Who "Protects" You or Makes Excuses for You Is Not Good for Your Career

In the long run, your career will suffer, and opportunities for advancement will be fewer. If you make a mistake, own it. We all make mistakes.

Lesson 2: Understand That If You Are Doing a Good Job, You Deserve to Be in That Job

A boss who talks about you behind your back, excusing your performance, is not doing you any favors. Quite the contrary. If you see this happening, speak to your boss and put a stop to it. Ask for their support. Corporate streetfighters are tough and competent; they do not need "protection."

CHAPTER 2:

TAKING CONTROL OF YOUR CAREER

ROUND 10

HAVE A PLAN FOR YOUR CAREER

When I was a CEO, I would have birthday lunches with the employees at each of our offices on the month of their birthday. This was something I had seen a prior CEO do, and I thought it was a great idea. These lunches gave employees unfettered access to ask me whatever they wanted and to get an honest answer from the CEO. It also gave me the opportunity to get unfettered access to the people who were actually doing the work to find out what was really going on in the company. The next two rounds will guide you on how to make the most of meetings with senior executives. In this round I will discuss how, as a corporate streetfighter, you can think strategically about your career.

Do you have a plan for your career? Career advancement and the opportunity for promotion was a frequent topic at these lunches. Often someone would ask how quickly we promote people or what the opportunities are for advancement in the company. In general when you are in a fast-growing company, there are many opportunities for advancement, but when there is little growth, there are far fewer opportunities. Having experienced both, my answers would vary depending on the situation.

When the subject came up, I would ask for a show of hands of how many people had a plan for where they would like to be in the organization five years from now. Almost no one raised their hand. When I pressed, the general answer was, "I would like to be promoted and to make more money."

I would respond, "Promoted to what?" Most of the people at these meetings were entry-level personnel or slightly above, and there were many departments in the company and opportunities for advancement.

I would try to find out if the employees had designs to work in a specific department and had a plan to make that happen, but generally, I learned that they were waiting for job postings on the internal website and that they would apply for almost any job that had a higher title and paid more money. They would then try to figure out if they truly liked the job or not.

Strive to find work that you are passionate about and where you feel you can make a difference.

This approach can lead to having a series of jobs, but it is not a good way to have a successful career. If you are ambitious, you should strive to find work that you are passionate about and where you feel you can make a difference. Most people do better at things they like to do, and certainly, there is a higher likelihood that you will be happier in all aspects of your life if you enjoy what you do at work. People also tend to perform better when doing work that they are passionate about.

One interesting note is that very few employees at any level in the company were doing a job that they majored in while in college.

Several were working at the company because friends of theirs recommended that they apply, and many were hesitant because they felt they had no background for the job. However, most companies cannot find people who have prior training for all of their entry-level jobs, creating a willingness to hire people who have a liberal arts degree and appear smart and motivated.

Therefore, if you are looking for your first or second job, don't limit yourself to what you studied in school. Look for industries that you would like to be a part of and apply. Once hired, you can see if you really want to remain in that industry, and then you should plot a course to the career you desire.

Looking for career advancement, many entry-level employees in the companies I ran aspired to be project managers. When asked how they planned to move from their present situation to project management, they had no idea or said that they would apply when an associate project manager job was posted and see what happened. The problem with that is there is nothing differentiating them from all the other entry-level employees who are doing exactly the same thing!

I suggested a different approach. Go to the director of project management and state your interest for being in that department someday (see round 15 on the importance of asking for what you want). Ask the director what online courses or reading you might do to better prepare you for the job. Ask if it would be OK for you to shadow someone on the job (on your own time) to learn more about the work and to better prepare yourself for the role.

CORPORATE STREETFIGHTER STRATEGY—BE PROACTIVE IN CHOOSING YOUR NEXT STEPS

Taking control of your career and destiny is something only you can do. You need to differentiate yourself from the crowd.

Lesson 1: Play the Long Game as You Look for Your First or Second Career Opportunity

Look for places you can have an exciting and fulfilling career, not just a job to pay the bills. The sooner you get started on a career path, the faster you will reach your goals.

Lesson 2: A Fast-Growth Company Offers More Opportunities

If career advancement is very important to you and you are good at what you do, a fast-growth company is much more likely to provide opportunities for advancement than a company that is solid, but growth is slow.

Lesson 3: There Is Nothing Wrong with Being Happy in the Role You Are Currently In

Not everyone is cut out to be in management. If you are happy with your job/company and being promoted is more of a plus than a necessity, there is nothing wrong with staying and having a career with that company. Most companies have ways of incentivizing steadfast employees.

Lesson 4: Be Proactive

Use your time at the company to identify departments you would like to work in or managers you would like to work for. Have a plan for your own advancement and do not rely on fate or wait for opportunities to arise.

Lesson 5: Once You Have a Plan, Act on It

Use the example given on project management as a road map. Importantly, please make sure that you are considered good at what you do in your current role before looking to move on, as you will want a positive recommendation from others in the company.

MAKING A GOOD FIRST IMPRESSION AND NEGOTIATING A SALARY WHEN STARTING A NEW JOB

When you have the chance to meet with executives in the company, it is important to make the most of those opportunities. This holds true from your first interview through any and all encounters you have with senior management. Making a good first impression is extremely important, as you only have one opportunity to *make* a first impression. As most executives value their own intuition and judgment, a good first impression can carry you through when a couple of things go wrong, but a bad first impression can turn a few minor infractions into a career disaster.

First, I'll talk about your initial job interview. Then I'll address what it takes to make an impression once you have the job.

THE INTERVIEW PROCESS

Do you come prepared to win when interviewing for a job? It amazes me how many people I have interviewed for executive jobs who have no idea about the company and what it does. They saw the job listing or had a call with a recruiter and just showed up for an interview. Most of these candidates have an uphill battle with me, as I fail to comprehend how they can interview for an executive job without taking any time to learn about the company and what we do. All it takes is a few clicks on the internet to get some cursory knowledge of the company and its culture.

Clearly, you can't be expected to know everything about a company just looking on the internet, so have some good questions prepared for the interviewers. Often you will meet the most senior executive in your last formal interview, so make sure to incorporate everything you learn in your prior interviews into the subsequent interviews you have.

You will be more and more knowledgeable as you progress through the process, and you will be able to sound quite well informed by the time your reach your final interview with the most senior person on the team. Needless to say, in the interview process, a good first impression is about all there is, as a decision will be made on how you presented yourself on that day.

Another thing about the interview process is that interviewers often think the interview went better when they, not you, do most of the talking. Perhaps there is a bias, and they are doing most of the talking when they really like your résumé, and they are trying to convince you to come on board, or maybe you just have less of a chance of a serious gaffe if you are doing less talking. But in any event, I have seen this happen many times.

I have seen the opposite happen when the interviewee takes five to ten minutes to answer just one question. In a thirty-minute interview, that is one-third of the time. I am sure the interviewer stopped really listening long before the candidate finished answering, and the entire flow of the interview will now be off-kilter, as the interviewer has lost interest. Please keep your answers short and to the point, a back-and-forth dialogue where you get to know a little bit about each other and how each of you thinks is best.

Do you struggle when you are interviewing and you are asked, "What compensation are you expecting?" You are not alone. If you want the job, you don't want to ask for so much that you price yourself out of the job. Of course, you want to get the best package you can. Note that I said *best package*, not best salary.

When it comes to negotiating your salary, companies are no longer allowed to ask how much you are currently making. That practice generally served to keep women and minorities at lower salaries, as the new company could offer you more than you are making now but less than others in that position are currently making. If they throw out a number, whether you like the number or not, let them know that you are interested in the job and that if an offer is made, you would like to hear the whole package and not just the salary. This approach is best to keep you in the running and at least get you a chance to get to the interview.

One of my favorite chess terms is *zugzwang*. When you put an opponent in zugzwang, it means that they have to make the next move, and no matter what move they make, *you win*. When discussing compensation, the most important thing is to never set up a situation where you are *negotiating against yourself*. So what should you do if you are offered the job and asked what compensation you are looking for?

SALARY AND CAREER

First, ask if there is a salary range for the position. If the range is more than you are making now, then you are starting in good shape. If less than you are making now, ask them if they are flexible on salary, but let them know that you are interested in the entire package.

Second, ask about bonuses and stock options. For bonuses, ask what percentage of your salary the bonus is and whether or not they have they been paid regularly in the past.

Third, ask about the chances for advancement in the company. You are interviewing for a job, but you want a career. A good financial package won't remain good if you have no opportunity for advancement.

BENEFITS

Fourth, ask about vacation time. Vacation time is compensation; if you are offered a similar salary but you get an extra week or two off, you are actually getting an increase.

Fifth, ask about healthcare. This is very important, and if you have never purchased healthcare on your own, you will find that it is really expensive. The amount the company pays toward your healthcare can fluctuate significantly, and the money you pay toward your healthcare comes out of your salary.

Finally, ask about a 401(k) or other savings plan and what percentage of your salary contribution the company matches. This varies greatly. Some companies don't match at all, and others will match 100 percent. Your contributions and the company match are tax-free. Younger people tend to consider 401(k)s as retirement income, and they want the money now, so their contributions tend to be small. My advice is put as much as you can into a 401(k). If you can put in $6,000 a year and the company matches 100 percent, you could be making an extra $8,000 a year, $2,000 in tax saving for you and $6,000 of free money from the company. This is *real compensation*, and many people pay no attention to this.

CORPORATE STREETFIGHTER STRATEGY— INTERVIEW AND NEGOTIATE LIKE A PRO

The interview is the beginning of your career at a company. Wowing them will not only land you the job but people also will have their eye on you for the future.

Lesson 1: Come Prepared

It is embarrassing to come to an interview and not know anything about the company. The easiest thing you can do is study the company's website. A simple internet search can often give you enough information to show you have done your due diligence.

Lesson 2: Use Each Interview to Advance Your Knowledge of the Job and the Company

You are learning from each person who interviews you. Your answers should therefore evolve as the process goes on, reflecting what you have learned.

Lesson 3: Keep Your Answers Concise and Let the Interviewer Speak

Generally, the more the interviewer speaks, the better they think the interview went. By being concise and precise, you are less likely to say something that turns the interviewer off, and the more the interviewer speaks, the more you learn for when you meet the next interviewer.

Lesson 4: Interview to Win the Job, Then Discuss Salary and Benefits

There are a lot of things to consider when accepting a job offer. A corporate streetfighter is thinking ahead and planning their course of attack from the moment they step into the ring. Don't fixate on salary alone when you are offered a job. See the whole chessboard.

"Hello, Bob, how's it going?"

"Good, thank you sir."

EXPOSURE TO EXECUTIVES AFTER YOU ARE HIRED

For the average worker in a company, your encounters with executives are few and far between. Executives can form long-lasting impressions of you based on those encounters that can range from very impressed to "Why is this person still allowed to work here?" How often have you bumped into an executive in the hallway or in an elevator and had absolutely nothing to say to them, even when they tried to strike up a conversation with you?

Impressing executives in brief encounters is always a great career move. If a promotion is available, your boss might be asked by their boss why you are not getting it, even though that executive knows little about you and even less about the others up for the job. If you are up for a raise, you are going to get it if your boss's boss has a good impression of you.

On the other hand, the opposite will happen if you make a poor impression. Your boss may have to defend the raise even if it is well earned. Unfortunately, some bosses are not comfortable taking on their superiors, and someone else who impressed an executive may get the promotion or raise that you deserved. Don't let that happen. Below are two situations that accentuate this point.

I used to travel to Europe frequently to work with salespeople. These trips would be planned weeks in advance, and the salespeople were supposed to make sure that my time was well used when I arrived. Too many times I would show up, and there would be very few meetings and lots of excuses.

It was clear to me that those salespeople were either unwilling or unable to do the work needed; thus, my impressions of them were poor. There was one salesperson who would tell me that he could fill my schedule at the last minute, if necessary, but preferably in advance. He would always be able to get me meetings, and we would book millions of dollars in business together. He was smart enough to realize the importance of getting me in front of his clients. To me he was the best salesperson we had in Europe. He was well prepared and had good client relationships.

However, often the best person at doing their job is not the best person to be promoted. We did lots of meetings together, but he never planned for any downtime or meals. Often we did a new city each day with flights every night. We were grabbing food at gas stations between meetings and arriving at hotels in the evening after the hotel restaurants had closed. This made these trips very hard on me and showed a lack of thought to these matters.

I complained that I was tired of being on so many flights and that he needed to try to maximize the number of clients (or prospective clients) we saw in each city, as the travel was a huge drain. On a subsequent trip, I was told "not to worry," as he had made sure that my flights were limited and had scheduled me to take a train where that was possible, as he knew that I wanted to avoid flights. Naturally,

I assumed that I would be stationed in a major city and be able to take a train to different venues around the city, which would comply with my request. Instead, on my second day, I got on the train and realized that I was on a six-hour train ride to a location I could have flown to in forty-five minutes. When I confronted the salesperson, he stated, "But you said that you wanted to limit the flights, so I put you on a train instead." I could not believe the ridiculousness of his logic in thinking that I would prefer a six-hour train ride to a forty-five-minute flight when the whole point of my request was to limit my travel time! This made it clear to me that he was not executive material, but he was still the best and most productive salesperson I had in Europe, and eventually, we found common ground.

In another instance I had an executive colleague who was good at his job, but every time he had the CEO's ear, he would take the opportunity to complain about his base compensation, his bonus, or his stock grants. The CEO would engage with him to hear about his performance and that of his division, but the conversation always evolved to money. The CEO came away with the impression that all this person cared about was money and that they had no interest in the company, its mission, or its people. Nothing could

You should never assume that executives are doing homework on you behind the scenes and really know what you are doing.

have been further from the truth, but when all you speak about is one thing, what else can you expect the CEO to think?

You should never assume that executives are doing homework on you behind the scenes and really know what you are doing. They are, however, likely to go to your boss after an encounter to try to reaffirm their positive or negative thinking about you. But I would not count on your boss being able to change the CEO's opinion once it is formed.

CORPORATE STREETFIGHTER STRATEGY—MAKE THE MOST OF CHANCE SENIOR EXECUTIVE ENCOUNTERS

What appear to be chance encounters can have a substantial impact on your career. Make the most of any encounter with a senior executive.

Lesson 1: Have an Elevator Speech Prepared

An elevator speech is a short blurb on what you would say about yourself and your job if asked in the time it takes an elevator to go from one floor to another. Memorizing this brief conversation will allow you to put your best foot forward and make a good impression when you get exposure to senior executives.

Lesson 2: Talk about Things That Are Important to the Business and Showcase Yourself

Don't waste an opportunity to impress an executive by complaining about the company or your boss. This will reflect poorly on you. Instead, be positive and cite examples where your actions were aligned with the company's mission and proved beneficial.

Lesson 3: Perception Is Reality

However you feel about yourself or how your boss feels about you, executives tend to remember interactions with people if they are impactful enough. This will lead to them having a positive inclination concerning your future career development.

YOUR FIRST JOB— HOW LONG SHOULD YOU STAY?

How long did you stay in your first job? Why did you leave? After taking my first industry (nondoctor) job, it became clear to me that my boss had "retired" into this job, and his primary motivation was to be left alone, collect good money and stock options, and by no means do anything that he could be blamed for or fired for. As a new employee who joined the company to make a difference, I was constantly being told what I should *not* be doing.

People in other departments encouraged me to continue to make inroads between the medical and marketing departments, but my boss monitored this carefully to make sure that I never did anything too far-reaching that might send some unwanted attention our way. I tried to play ball; after all my boss was intelligent and seemed to know the corporate culture, but I had a colleague who, like me, came to make a difference and who was continuously butting heads with the boss.

One day after a long shouting match, my colleague was told that he could not work on a project that could make hundreds of millions for the company because the risk of failure was too great. He promptly went to the marketing department and pitched his idea to them, and they loved it. As there is little money in the medical department and a lot of money in the marketing department, they generally get their way. Soon some VPs of marketing were calling my boss to congratulate him on the great idea his department had come up with.

Shortly thereafter, there was yelling of increased intensity between my colleague and our boss, as now his hand was forced. My colleague's only request was that the boss let me assist him, as there was a cardiology aspect to the project. The boss agreed if I was so foolhardy to take the project on, but foolhardy I was because I was desperate to make a difference.

The end result was that the project was a great success, and a meeting was held in Europe (you could do that in the old days) to which all the important physicians who had contributed to our knowledge in this area were invited. My colleague and I went all over the country training these speakers for the meeting, and the marketing department told our boss that they were giving him the ability to bring two people from our department to the meeting as a reward for our work. You guessed it; he brought two of his buddies, and we were not invited. We appealed to marketing, but there was nothing they could do across company lines.

Several months later our boss was given a promotion, a raise, and a bonus. He gave us a promotion that we were promised months earlier but no significant raise and no bonus. He explained that although the project was a success, we had disobeyed him and put him at risk, and he felt that it would not be appropriate to reward us. Of course, *he* had no problem being rewarded.

My colleague was more furious than I was, and every day he would remind me how miserable it was to be working at this company.

But listening to his complaining got me so worked up that I ended up quitting before him! Being the newbies that we were, we decided that the company was much too slow-moving, that they did not reward innovation, that the higher-ups clearly did not know what they were doing, and that we had to move on.

As years passed, being a self-reflective type, I realized that although I disagreed with our boss's approach, he clearly understood the organization that he was working in and how to keep his job for the long term. He was advising us to behave as he would so that we all could have easy lives without concern for our jobs. The problem was that my colleague and I did not come to the company to have easy lives without fear of being fired. We came to *accomplish* something.

As I moved on in my career and hired several people either directly out of college or from jobs that were not corporate in nature, I saw that many decided to leave the company after a few years. In some cases it was because other opportunities arose that were just too good to pass up. However, even those who stayed would complain that the corporation really didn't care about them or that they were not promoted fast enough or that management had no idea what they were doing and other statements of unhappiness. As I had harbored some similar feelings in my

Those with the least knowledge always seem to think they know the most, and the more you learn, the more you realize how much you do not know.

first job, I wasn't shocked by this, but I was surprised by the regularity with which these sentiments repeated themselves.

I did my best to keep in touch with people and came to see that these feelings were part of the growing pains of being in a business for the first time and not understanding all of the complications involved.

Surely, they were correct that the company could have operated better, but just about any place can operate better than it does. However, those with the least knowledge always seem to think they know the most, and the more you learn, the more you realize how much you do not know.

Many of the people who moved on to other places discovered that if the people running our company were incompetent, the people running their new company were blithering idiots in comparison! This prompted many to move on to yet a third opportunity where, by most accounts, things were similar to our company. So they found themselves back in a company similar to ours but still at an entry-level position or one just above it, whereas if they had stayed with us, they would likely have already been promoted to a higher position and would be making more money.

Trying to intervene in this process, I started discussing this with new hires, assuring them that, after a couple of years, they would likely decide that the company and myself did not know what was going on and that they could not stay here any longer. Over time I reviewed what I had learned with them in the hope of increasing retention by helping them avoid the pitfalls of others. But as all of us who are parents have learned, we can try to teach our children to avoid the mistakes that we have made, but generally, they need to learn those lessons for themselves.

The same has generally been true in business, and I found very few who were willing to learn from the experience of others. I have always found it gratifying when years later, after achieving managerial or executive status, people would come back to me and say they remembered our conversation well and not giving it its due, and now they try to duplicate my efforts with their employees because they have had similar experiences. I then wish them luck and tell them

I hope they will be more successful with their employees than I was with them!

CORPORATE STREETFIGHTER STRATEGY—MAKE SURE THAT THE GRASS IS INDEED GREENER BEFORE YOU GO

Generally, those with the least knowledge and experience think they know more than the executives in a company because they do not *know* what they do not know and how much there is to know!

Lesson 1: The Grass Is Not Always Greener Elsewhere

Talk to friends about their working experiences and compare those with the culture in your place of employment. How much are you learning? Are you treated well? Are your salary and benefits comparable to others? What is the opportunity for career growth? Do not be too quick to judge the company leadership.

Lesson 2: Your Knowledge Is Portable

When I first joined the corporate world, people tended to join a company and plan for a career there. The companies were more loyal to the employees back then and vice versa. The world has changed, and people change jobs frequently but not always for the right reasons. There is always either a push (don't like it where you are, don't like your salary, don't like your boss) or a pull (better career, better salary, better boss) or some combination of the two. If you are going to change jobs, take positions that promote your intellectual growth and increase your responsibilities. Think more about the career you are building than about the job.

ROUND 14

IF YOU WANT THE PROMOTION, ASK FOR IT (ESPECIALLY IN SALES AND MARKETING)

Have you ever watched someone else get the promotion that you thought was yours? One of the most important lessons I learned early on in my career was that "the squeaky wheel gets the grease" or that if you want something, you are more likely to get it if you *ask* for it.

The Bible says, "The Lord is good to those who wait," and this has likely led to the saying "Good things come to those who wait." However, this certainly is not true in business!

> **If you want something, you are more likely to get it if you ask for it.**

A quote that has been attributed to Lincoln, but since disproven, is more applicable: "Good things come to those who wait but only those left behind by those that hustle!" I must admit I was taken aback the first time I saw this in practice.

There was a promotion available in marketing, and I had worked with just about all of the product leads who were contenders for the job. To me there was a clear favorite. One product lead was just more intelligent, more knowledgeable, and more successful with his product line than the rest. As far as I was concerned, it was a foregone conclusion that he would get the job. (And perhaps it was to him as well.) Instead, the promotion went to another member of the team who was certainly better politically connected and very likable but did not seem to be at the level of the person I expected to get the job. Being inquisitive and fairly new to the business world and having great respect and a good relationship with the executive doing the promoting, I engaged him in a conversation that went something like this:

> **ME:** Can I ask why Person Y got the promotion and not Person X, as in my opinion Person X was far more qualified?
>
> **EXECUTIVE:** The answer is simple. Person Y never asked to be considered for the promotion.
>
> **ME:** Should someone really have to ask for a promotion when their work demonstrates that the individual is highly qualified and deserves the promotion?
>
> **EXECUTIVE:** Jeff, I run a sales and marketing department. If a person cannot or does not sell themselves and their abilities within the company, how can I expect them to do it outside of the company? Person Y came to me and made a good case as to why he should get the job and described how he would do the job if he got it. Person X never asked for or expressed interest in the promotion, even though you and I both know he wanted it.

As this was indeed a sales and marketing department, I did see the executive's point, but it still struck me as unfair. However, over time I noticed that this was not unique to sales and marketing.

If you want to advance, you should make it known that you want to advance. If there is an opening or you believe there will be an opportunity for advancement in the near future and you are interested in it, you should apply for it. Make it known to your boss that you want the job. It seems so obvious, but this frequently goes undone.

Later in my career, I saw a similar situation unfold. Two sales executives were vying for a recently vacated position as head of sales. One of the executives had a team that was performing at or better than the level expected of them, but the executive did not show a lot of energy and did not lobby for the position. This executive felt that he had earned the position by the performance of his team and that it was sufficient. He never asked for any assistance in trying to obtain the position. He knew he would be interviewed for the position and awaited that day with the confidence that his record would speak for itself. With that mindset he fully expected to get the job.

The other executive came to see me frequently and asked questions as to the type of leader the CEO was looking for. He bounced a lot of his ideas off me and then honed them before scheduling meetings with the CEO to discuss his plans and strategy for the sales department. He had a much more outgoing personality than the other candidate, and he peppered the CEO with his ideas and brainstormed different ways to grow the business. Before the formal interview process had begun, he had already secured the job. The other candidate had no chance and was greatly disappointed that his performance alone was not enough. He missed the point that, at the highest levels, strategy, leadership, and initiative are also very important factors for career growth.

On the opposite side of the coin, if there have been several openings and you have never been promoted, you need to realize that there is a reason, and that reason is not likely to go away by itself. I would suggest that you meet with your boss to understand the reason that you are being passed over. These conversations are not always pleasant for either party, but if you do not have that conversation, you will remain in the dark. If you are told that your abilities, work ethic, or attitude are not up to par, try to work with your boss to put a plan together for you to improve.

However, when most people are told that they are lacking in any of the areas previously mentioned, they just get angry with the boss and disagree. After all you know that you deserved that promotion! But I would suggest that self-reflection is a good thing, and even if you think that the boss has the wrong perception of you, it is likely that you are doing something that is giving the boss that perception. See round 5 on how the worst boss forced me to develop the skills for success for an example.

One of the most interesting phenomena is what I would call the "What came first, the chicken or the egg?" approach to asking for a promotion. Employees will go to their manager and say that they feel they have been in their current job too long, and they want a promotion. Good managers should address the employee's concerns and explain what it will take for them to achieve the next level, where they are at currently, and what they need to show to move up. A worthy employee will then work out a plan with their manager to achieve those milestones with the promise of a promotion if they are achieved in a given period.

However, there are other employees who respond, "Why should I do all of that extra work without getting the promotion? Promote me, and then I will do the work." If your manager has taken the time to explain to you the work, attitude, and results that they would like to see to make the promotion happen, then you should follow through, show the results, and then ask for the promotion you now deserve. Saying that you feel that it is extra work sends negative signals. Why would a manager promote someone who wants the reward prior to doing the work when there are so many people who are doing the work because they care about the company and their jobs? As a matter of fact, your manager was discussing a promotion with you because they thought that was how you felt, but you have now convinced them that they were wrong and that what you really care about is having a higher title and more money.

You could leave the impression that you don't care about doing what it takes to get there and to be successful. In these cases the employee may never get that promotion, especially if this conversation has happened more than once. The employee will become frustrated and seek the promotion elsewhere, and they will probably get it. Unfortunately, for the new company, the work ethic of the employee probably won't match the new title and expectations.

CORPORATE STREETFIGHTER STRATEGY—MAKE YOUR INTEREST IN PROMOTIONS KNOWN AND TELL YOUR BOSS WHY YOU HAVE WHAT IT TAKES TO GET IT

Hope is not a plan! Do not wait for good things to happen for you, even if you feel you deserve them. Be proactive regarding your career advancement.

Lesson 1: Show Your Interest in the Position When It Becomes Available

Speak to the hiring managers and human resources (human capital management in some workplaces). Find out the requirements for the job and what they are looking for in an individual. Show them that you are *that person*. Leave as little to chance as you can. Also, show your interest in remaining with the company and the contribution you will make to the company. Promotions are not just all about you. You will be expected to deliver for the business. Show that you understand that.

Lesson 2: If You Feel You Are Deserving of Advancement and a Suitable Position Is Available, You Should Ask for the Job

This accomplishes several things:

1. It puts people on notice that you want the job, and therefore, you will likely be displeased if you do not get it.

2. It will increase your chances of getting the job, as perhaps you were under the radar, or one of your coworkers has been busy lobbying for the promotion.

3. If your manager thinks you are not ready for the promotion but thinks highly of you, the manager should address the situation with you and explain what it will take for you to make it to the next level and how and when that might happen.

4. If your manager is not the type of person to address the above with you, it gives you a chance to address it with your manager.

5. Finally, if you were well qualified but beaten out for the promotion by someone else who is either more qualified or has a lot more experience, the company may try to temper the blow by giving you a raise and/or a smaller promotion to keep you engaged and interested in remaining with the company.

Lesson 3: If You Keep Getting Passed Over for Promotions, Some Self-Assessment Is in Order

Have a frank discussion with your boss as to what you may be missing or lacking and how they would rate your performance. You may disagree with the assessment that is made of you, but that perception is the other person's reality, and it needs to be addressed. I can say with certainty that people notice when an employee changes the way they interact with their team and with management. This can often be accomplished with coaching, and being noticed is an important part of advancement.

> You may disagree with the assessment that is made of you, but that perception is the other person's reality, and it needs to be addressed.

I have seen a few circumstances where someone has fallen under the radar due to changes in management or because they are just a quiet person who does a good job. In those cases it is generally in management's best interest to accommodate that person's request for a promotion or a raise.

Lesson 4: Don't Make Getting a Promotion a Condition of Getting the Work Done

Several times (and this has been especially true in Europe) I have been told that an employee would be more than happy to do all the things requested if, and only if, they receive a promotion. I advise all readers of this book not to take this approach. If your manager takes the time to explain to you what you need to do to get a promotion, do the work and hold them to their word.

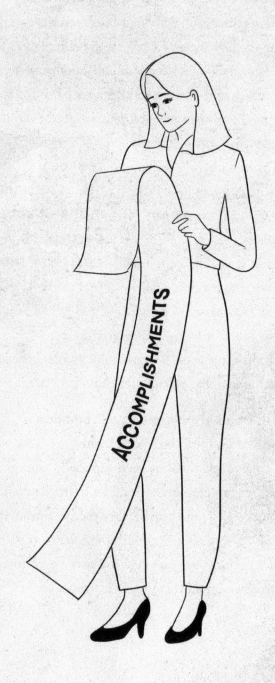

ASKING FOR A RAISE OR A BONUS

Are you comfortable going to your boss and asking for a raise? Do you know the difference between a real raise and an annual adjustment? Most companies have standard cost of living adjustments (COLA) that they apply every year to match inflation. Basically, these "raises" are routine and meant to ensure that your spending power remains constant year over year. When you get your annual review, you receive this adjustment, and you feel you just got a raise. But this really isn't a raise. A raise is an additional increase you receive over and above the COLA.

In addition to raises, some companies reward employees with "spot bonuses." These are designed to recognize you when your work goes beyond the call of duty to get things done or for a new idea, but that work is not deemed to be worthy of a promotion. Bonuses can also replace raises in situations where the company has a salary band for job titles, and they work diligently to make sure that all employees doing a similar job are compensated within that salary range.

So what about a real raise that may or may not come with a promotion? If you are lucky, you work in an environment where the higher-ups recognize what you bring to the table and want to reward you for your work and also to retain you as an employee. If you do not work in such an environment, you need to ask yourself, "What is the best way and the best time for me to approach my boss for a raise or a spot bonus?" assuming, of course, you deserve one! Let's start with the simple ones.

1. You have been working at the company for several years, and they just hired someone new to do the same job you do. You learned they are making more than you are. Although management often discourages employees from discussing salaries, we know this goes on all the time. If you bring this up to your boss or human resources, you should be compensated appropriately and perhaps ask for a bit more because you have more years of experience than the new hire.

2. You did not get a COLA increase in the prior year because the company was doing poorly, but now the company is doing well, and there has been no mention of an increase. At a minimum you should ask for the COLA increase. The company is now doing well, and you sacrificed in the prior year. It would also be reasonable to ask to be made whole for the COLA increase that you sacrificed in the prior year, as the company is now back on track, and you should be rewarded for your loyalty.

3. You put in a significant amount of overtime on a project that proved very successful for the company, and you did not receive a financial reward. This is what spot bonuses were designed for. It is perfectly reasonable to ask for some additional reward for your work. After all what will happen the next time they need you to go the extra mile if they don't acknowledge your work this time?

4. You come up with an idea that closes a deal or helps the company create a successful new product. If your idea closes a significant new deal that would not have otherwise sold, this is what spot bonuses are also made for. If your idea results in a successful new product, a spot bonus should be the minimum you receive.

WHAT ABOUT THREATENING TO RESIGN?

In my opinion threatening to resign is almost always a bad idea. It is an especially bad idea if you have no other opportunities lined up. In threatening to resign, you are working under the premise that the company will have difficulty getting along without you. Perhaps the company will even go under without you. Even at the highest levels of an organization, I have rarely seen that happen. The company just keeps moving on when you move on, and you need to make sure that you do not hurt yourself more than you hurt the company by leaving.

What you can do is search the market for another opportunity that pays more. In the past this would be done by working with recruiters, especially at the C-suite level. But for many people and positions, most of the information you need is easily available online.

If you get a good offer and you would really rather stay where you are, then you can use that offer as leverage with the understanding that the company may not choose to, or be able to, make you a competitive counteroffer. In many cases you will be convinced to stay, and several months later, a recruiter from one of the companies you found online will call you with an opportunity that you can't refuse, and you will move on. If your boss has seen this situation several times, as I have, the boss may not be inclined to try to save anyone who wants to leave, as they know it is likely that they are just kicking the can down the road, and they will need to find a suitable replacement for you at some point in the future.

CORPORATE STREETFIGHTER STRATEGY— MAKE SURE THAT YOU ARE APPROPRIATELY REWARDED AND RECOGNIZED FOR YOUR WORK

You should be compensated for your performance. A corporate street-fighter asks for promotions. They are confident in asking for a raise. In addition to financial compensation, recognition of achievements with commensurate career growth is important.

Lesson 1: Speak Up

Many bosses are not good about verbally acknowledging people's work, let alone providing a financial reward for what is done. By asking for what you deserve, the worst that can happen is that you are told no, and then you need to reassess if this is a place you want to spend your career. However, in many cases no one has thought about a financial reward, but now that you mentioned it, they will see that there is merit to your suggestion.

Lesson 2: Don't Let Yourself or Your Work Be Taken for Granted

If you have come up with and *implemented* ideas that have taken the business to a new level of revenue or profitability, you should be entitled to substantial financial compensation. This may be a promotion, raise, stock, or profit sharing. Also, you should not have to put up with a boss who presents your ideas as their own. I have always given credit where credit is due, and I have respected my subordinates when they come to me and tell me that the idea came from one of their employees as opposed to themselves. Your career will likely stagnate working for a boss who does not credit you for your work, and this is a good indicator that you will likely be better off elsewhere.

Lesson 3: Don't Threaten to Quit without Another Acceptable Offer in Hand

You may find yourself out of a job. It is essential to have a backup plan. Bluffing can work against you, so make sure you have other opportunities lined up.

Lesson 4: Truly Understand Why You Want to Leave Your Job

If you are looking to leave the company for lack of raises or promotions, be sure that is the real and perhaps only reason you want to leave. As that is rarely the case, it might make sense to just move on to another opportunity. The circumstances outside of your upward mobility may not be the main factors of your discontent, but perhaps they are just a justification for you to stay in a position that is no longer suitable for you.

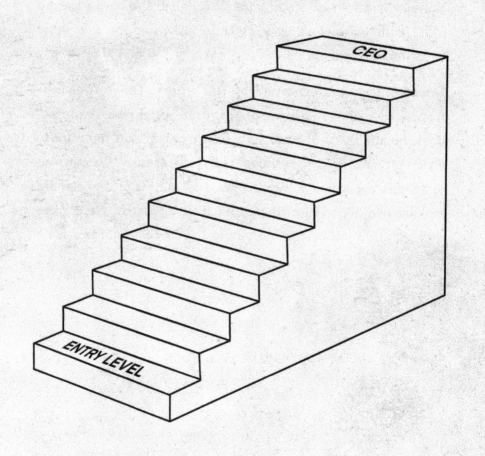

ROUND 16

STAGES OF CAREER ADVANCEMENT

In this round I have outlined the skills that I feel employees need to possess to achieve a certain level of responsibility in the corporate world. The responsibilities and skills below are not a standard but the characteristics I would expect of corporate streetfighters. Be aware that some companies have notoriously high or low titles, and that should be taken into account when reviewing the below. Are you aware of the titles, positions, and responsibilities of the different roles in your company?

Entry-Level Worker: For most people this is your first job. You are starting at or near the bottom of the corporate ladder. It is expected that you will show up every day on time, put in a full day's work, be productive, and do a good job. Putting in some extra time when needed, taking initiative, and having some ideas are all extras that will get you noticed. You will also get noticed if you are the most productive worker in the group.

Supervisor: Generally, the person who gets this job comes from the group who gets noticed as an entry-level worker. Just because you are the best worker does not mean you will be a good supervisor. But in a purely operational environment, if you are the best worker and can teach others to approach your level of performance, then you should be a candidate for promotion. Certainly, if you are the best worker and you possess the initiative and drive mentioned above, in addition to your work product, you should be a prime candidate for a supervisor role. Often the promotion goes to someone who is willing to go the extra mile and has become an asset to the boss.

In the next round, we will discuss the difficulties of your first promotion, and you will see that it can be very demanding both professionally and personally. It is important that you recognize this before jumping in. As far as skill level goes, I would say that most supervisors should be good at identifying problems in the area where they are assigned and bringing them to their manager's attention.

As you have just come from a line job, you should already have a good idea of some things that should be fixed and done better. You will now have a chance to examine the work of your ex-coworkers, and you will definitely find things that they need to improve on. Gaining their trust while helping them improve their performance will also help you on your way to your next promotion, and hopefully, that will result in one of them stepping up their game so they can take your job when you move up. After all you will do better after you are promoted to manager if there is someone in your old supervisor role who will make you look good!

Complaining about a problem without posing a solution is called whining.

—THEODORE ROOSEVELT

Manager: As a manager you should be capable of managing both processes and people. You should work with the supervisor and use metrics to identify the most and least productive workers on your team. Top performers should be rewarded, and you should avoid supplementing the weak performance of poor performers by heaping work on your best performers. Instead, you should work with low producers to improve their performance, and if that fails, you should replace them.

Strong performance should be a balance of productivity and quality. Many people will say that they work slowly to ensure high quality, but my experience has generally shown the opposite. Paradoxically, my most productive people have also made the fewest errors.

The main goals in this job are to keep the workplace productive, to keep the high performers happy with praise and recognition, and to coach those who are not performing to improve their performance and, if necessary, replace them if they are not responsive to performance improvement plans. In my experience most performance-based teams look like the following:

- **5 percent superhigh performers:** When it comes to productivity, these people are on a different level. In a small group there may only be one person who fits the bill. They will often produce 50 percent more than an average performer and more than double of a below-average performer.

- **10 percent high performers:** This group generally delivers 10 percent to 25 percent more than the expected workload on a consistent basis.

- **65 percent average performers:** This group is the backbone of any company, and companies cannot function without them. They perform 90 percent to 110 percent of the expected workload on a consistent basis, and they care about their job and the company. Very few people from this group will evolve to a higher level in the corporation, but as a manager, you must find a way to keep this group engaged.

- ✊ **20 percent below-average performers:** Yes, I know this seems like a high number, and many of you reading this will say that it is not true where you work, but then I would say that you are not using adequate metrics. All too often I have seen below-average performers who are darlings of management due to their personalities.

In one company I instituted metrics over the strong objections of the division manager. The manager was promoted through the ranks of that division and knew every person personally and was convinced there was nothing to be learned by measuring performance that she did not already know. She felt that doing the documentation would be cumbersome to the team and slow their performance. Rather than arguing the issue further, we agreed on a two-week test. If I was proved correct, we would continue to measure performance, and if she was proved correct, we would stop. At that time, she was considering firing a long-term employee whom she felt had become unhelpful due to his seniority and replacing him with a younger employee who was always willing to help out when needed.

Well, after the two-week test, she came to my office in tears, as almost everything she thought to be true was not true. The person she wanted to fire was no longer helpful because every time someone left the team, he would quietly pick up more work. When we measured performance, he was doing three times the work of an average performer. No wonder he had no time to be helpful; he was swamped with work, and she had no idea. The employee who was Mr. Helpful was doing 50 percent of the work of an average person.

Obviously, she did not know what was really going on, and the supervisor below her didn't either. They relied completely on observation, gut, and intuition and not on measurement. If they fired the long-term worker, they would have needed three to four people to take his place due to his experience.

The solution was to take Mr. Helpful and have him work for the long-term employee who was almost fired as well as hiring one more person for that team. The best part of the story is that the manager went from a metrics blocker to a metrics zealot, and within a year, she had almost doubled the productivity of her team. This led to her promotion to director and eventually vice president.

Director: When you make it to the director level, you are now making the move from line management to an entry-level senior management position. (This should not be confused with titles like managing director, which are often very senior roles.) At this level you may have a couple of managers reporting to you and a couple of projects to work on, or you might only have one manager and one project. With the former you have really advanced your responsibility. With the latter you have advanced your title and your salary, but your responsibility will be more of a role in which you report what is going on to the higher-ups, and they tell you what strategies they want to enact.

Your job as director will be to make sure the work gets done and to be accountable to management. Unlike the roles of supervisor and manager, who should be adept at identifying problems, the director should come up with the solutions to those problems and also should be able to instruct the team on how to drive better performance from both quantity and quality perspectives. If you are in an organization

149

that is "political" in nature, this will be the job where your eyes will be opened to some of what is going on behind the scenes.

This position often reports to a vice president, and there will be times you will be asked to do things because the higher-ups demand it. Even though you know the team better than those above you, you may not be consulted on the approach taken. At this level you are a junior executive in the company, and if you have a dissenting opinion on the strategy being passed down, you should voice your concern to your boss. If there is a disagreement, you should be entitled to know why your plan is less compelling, as it will help you learn.

It is important to note that your opinions will have the greatest merit when they involve solving issues within your own department. At this level you should not try to change corporate strategy, as that needs to come from the top, and everyone needs to row in the same direction once the strategy is set.

Vice President: As a vice president, you should be coming up with new ideas to drive your line of the business forward and mentoring the directors who are your direct reports so that at least one of them will be able to step into your role someday. Moving to vice president is a major career step.

I once worked with a very talented individual who was a senior director for many years. I knew that he had been offered assistant vice president and vice president jobs and had turned them down. As I was highly motivated to move up the ranks, I was surprised and curious as to why he was not. When asked, he told me that there are lots of director jobs out there, and he felt that gave him extreme mobility to pursue positions he may want in the future, but there were much fewer vice president jobs. He felt that if you have been a vice president and choose to interview for a director position, people will ask why you are taking a step backward or not offer you the job at all. They might feel that you are just desperate for a job right now but will leave as soon as you find a more suitable position. I would say that in the large company environment we were in at the time, he was probably correct, but if you are a vice president in a smaller company, it is more likely than not that if you go to a larger company, you will enter at a director level.

Vice presidents should be able to motivate their teams and come up with new ideas to *grow* the business. They should still be close enough to the people in the line jobs and the sales team to understand what is working and what is not and to analytically determine why. Then by meeting with the appropriate members of the staff, they should be able to come up with new strategic directions to present to the C-suite.

Your presentations must be crisp and to the point. Start out by telling them what you are going to tell them, then tell them, and then close by reminding them of the key points you told them. There should be no doubt as to what your plan is, when it will begin, what will be needed to make it happen, how it will happen, how much it will cost, and most importantly what the result will be. That result can be increased sales and revenue, better quality, greater efficiency (less cost or more production), or anything else that might drive the business forward.

Those in the C-suite should be watching and coaching you to see if you have what it takes to join the C-suite in the future. The leap from vice president to the C-suite is one of the toughest to make, as there aren't many seats in the C-suite. Following the example above, if there are fewer vice president jobs than director jobs, there are certainly a lot fewer jobs in the C-suite.

C-Suite: Individuals in the C-suite should be operating on a different strategic level. They should be setting the course for business growth and profitability. This can be done in many ways including driving product and sales innovation, identifying potential acquisitions and mergers and making them happen, ensuring there is accountability for delivering for the company and for customers, and mentoring the future leaders of the company. Although there are many roles in the C-suite, I am only going to focus on the COO and CEO.

Chief Operating Officer: The chief operating officer makes sure the company runs smoothly. Often but not always, the CEO has a background in sales or has a proven track record in growing the revenue of businesses. The COO role is often taken by someone who has come up through the ranks on the operating side. As there are salespeople who understand operations and operators who can sell, the COO should be at the top of the shortlist if the CEO departs. In the best of organizations, the COO is the partner and copilot for the CEO. They should divide up the work based on their skill sets and work as a team to get the best out of the company's employees and to drive the growth of the business.

Having a proclivity to fix things, I have held this role several times. It can be extremely rewarding if the CEO gives direction but lets you use your skills to do the job. It can be extremely frustrating if the CEO is removed from the day to day but insists on telling you what needs to be done based on their beliefs without any facts. Whatever the situation is, it is important that the CEO and COO feel comfortable voicing their opinions to each other to resolve any issues amicably and in the best interest of the company.

Chief Executive Officer: The CEO sets the culture and direction of the entire organization. I have seen CEOs with a tremendous work ethic inspire the troops to follow along as the CEO rolls up their sleeves and leads by example. Other CEOs achieve the same outcome by being inspirational speakers. The power of the culture of an organization cannot be underestimated. There are companies where people love to come to work.

This job is about delivering on the financial and sales goals and keeping your most valuable employees happy and engaged. I used to tell my wife that if I played golf all day and the numbers were great, I would be a genius and a hero, but if I worked 24/7 and didn't deliver the numbers, then I would be an idiot and a loser. This was hard for her to accept, but if you don't want to be judged on what you deliver financially compared with how hard you work, do not take a CEO job.

Being a CEO was not something I aspired to do. So why did I take a CEO job in the first place? I never sought the CEO position and was generally happy being a part of the C-suite and making my contribution to the company. However, I do like fixing things when they are not working, and my company, which had been operating quite smoothly, suddenly became a fixer-upper.

When that happened, I felt I was uniquely qualified to get the company out of the situation it was in. As I had been a COO several times, thus doing the majority of the day-to-day work, I felt that it was just a small leap to the CEO position. What I had not counted on was the extra burden I put on myself, as now all final decisions would come from me. The pressure of knowing that you are responsible for the employment of thousands of people is huge when you are a person who cares. Also, you have now been elevated above your peers, and you sit between them and their issues and the board and their issues.

I find being a CEO to be one of the loneliest jobs there is. Fortunately, I have found that most CEOs seem to think alike, and meeting other CEOs was one way to see that there are a lot of intelligent, motivated, and creative people out there who are sitting in the same seat and share many of the same experiences.

So why would anyone want this job? I have heard many reasons, but most have to do with ego, money, power, proof of achievement, or some combination thereof. To me the right reason is to make the company better. I will admit that it does take some degree of ego to believe that you will make the company better, and that is OK. And if you do make the company better, certainly, you should be well compensated for it.

CORPORATE STREETFIGHTER STRATEGY— KNOW THE SKILL SET YOU NEED TO MOVE UP TO THE NEXT POSITION IN YOUR SIGHTS

It is important to know what is expected of you in the workplace. I have endeavored to give you an idea of my expectations for the most common corporate roles so you can apply your skills as a corporate streetfighter to move up the corporate ladder.

Lesson 1: Understand What It Takes to Hold a Certain Role in Your Company

Evaluate the criteria I set forward above and see if you are delivering in your current role. You want to be sure that you are performing in an exceptional and noticeable manner.

Lesson 2: Assess Your Skill Set to See If You Are Ready to Move Up

By understanding what will be expected, you can best judge whether you have what it takes or still have some work to do in order to be successful at the next rung of the corporate ladder.

YOUR FIRST PROMOTION

For many of you who are just starting out, this is the topic you are most interested in. In the current corporate environment, after a couple of years at a job, most people feel that they should get a promotion. Note that I did not say *deserve* a promotion. However, there are promotions, and there are *promotions*. You can be promoted from a level 1 worker to a level 2 worker, which is nice and generally comes with a raise, or you can be promoted to a supervisor, which is what we will focus on here.

As discussed in an earlier round, the best opportunities for swift career growth are with companies that are rapidly growing. When joining a company, it is important to get an understanding of what the career growth opportunities are (assuming you have some idea as to what you want to do) and what the company's growth prospects are. If you have joined a company because you need a job but not for the career opportunity, use your time there to understand the business and see where you want to be in the future. If there is nothing that suits you, you should move on unless you are happy staying at the level you are at.

I always tell people that the first promotion to supervisor is the hardest. Up to that point, you were one of the guys or gals going out after work and complaining about the company and/or the boss over drinks, but *you are now the boss*. Almost immediately things change. You are now on the road to career advancement, and you are responsible for not only your own work but also the work of those who were your peers or friends the day before.

Often the best worker is promoted to supervisor, but just as often, the best worker is not necessarily the best person to be a supervisor. When the best worker is promoted, the boss just lost their best worker, and it is likely that the person hired to replace the new supervisor will take a long time to reach that level of productivity if they reach it at all.

So if you are the new supervisor, you are starting with less productivity than your boss had. In addition, you have to deal with the usual hard feelings as to why you got the job versus your coworkers, and that can result in some slacking off a bit. When that happens, guess who has to encourage and perhaps discipline those who are no longer pulling their weight? *Yes*, it's you!

Congratulations, new supervisor! With no training in management and with a less productive staff, you have to figure out how to motivate and reinvigorate your team. If your goal in life is to be *liked* by everyone, don't take the promotion because you are doomed to failure. If people choose not to like you, that is their prerogative, but they absolutely must respect you and what you do.

So how do you navigate this minefield? The easiest way is if your boss is a mentor. I met with my direct reports weekly to ensure that they had clear direction and had the ability to ask any questions they needed to in order to learn the ropes as a new supervisor or to expand their knowledge if they had been doing it for a while. Your boss needs to give you clear direction as to what the priorities are and what metrics and deadlines need to be met. Your boss can also help you by sharing prior productivity metrics for your team and discussing their opinion of the work produced by your ex-peers. This can be very enlightening.

If your boss is not a mentor, then you should be proactive and ask for clear direction including priorities, what metrics to use, and the deadline you have to meet. As your current employees were once your peers, you should know their personalities and what motivates them better than your boss did, and you should use this information.

In addition to your native abilities, there were probably some habits and perhaps some tricks that you used to make yourself more productive that you can share with the team. After all as you were just doing their job and doing it well, you should be able to bring something to the table that the prior boss could not.

Ultimately, you will find that it is very difficult to be responsible for the work of others, especially since many of them do not have your work ethic or your talents. After all if they did, they might be getting the promotion instead of you. You have to come to accept that this is the case and do your best to mentor, coach, and motivate your team to be the most productive they can be. Hopefully, as part of that process, you will find that there are a couple of people who could have the potential to be you someday, so when you get your next promotion, you will have people you can rely on.

In a world where many people are worried about competition from subordinates, it is important to note that it will be hard for you to be promoted if you have no one to replace you in your current job

If you are not grooming a successor, you are not doing your job to its fullest.

as a supervisor. And if you are promoted, you will have no one to rely on to ensure your success. I would say that whatever level you are on the management scale (including and up to the CEO level), if you are not grooming a successor, you are not doing your job to its fullest.

CORPORATE STREETFIGHTER STRATEGY—MAKE THE MINDSET SHIFT FROM BEING AN INDIVIDUAL CONTRIBUTOR TO GETTING RESULTS THROUGH OTHERS

Your first promotion can be the hardest. You are now responsible for the work of others for the first time. You will have to hire new employees and discipline and perhaps fire those who were your peers.

Lesson 1: Go into Your First Supervisory Role with Your Eyes Open

Congratulations on being recognized for your work, but understand that there is a major difference between being an individual contributor and a boss.

Lesson 2: Learn from Others

If your boss is a mentor, be thankful and learn as much as you can. Also, look around the organization for other leaders you respect to see how they manage their teams.

Lesson 3: Treat Each Employee as an Individual

They are not you! If they were you, they would be getting the promotion you just got. Find out what motivates them and how to get the best out of them. Find the best of the group and start grooming them so you can move up to the next level when the time comes.

ROUND 18

FORGET ABOUT BEING LIKED— RESPECT IS BETTER

As discussed in the previous round, it can be difficult when you move up the chain and feel that people no longer like you because you have become a boss versus a peer or a friend. You need to get over that!

Your coworkers will undoubtedly treat you differently. In an attempt to show that you are still part of the crowd, you may make an extra effort to be liked by doing things that benefit certain employees but do not benefit the company. Avoid this trap at all costs!

I can assure you that you will not be liked any more than you are now, people will notice that you are playing favorites, and productivity will drop, as people will feel that they can take advantage of your good nature. And at some point, you may be faced with having to fire one of these people for poor performance, making you worse off than if you had just done the right thing in the first place.

I like to have a good relationship with everyone, but that is not my primary role in the business. We can be friendly over beers after work. At work I need you to do well at your job, and I will always reward people who do a great job. If an ex-peer is now your boss, please suppress any jealousy and just help them be successful.

If you do a great job, your time will come. If you don't, you will be stuck where you are, and that can result in years of bitterness culminating in your departure from a company where you could have had a rewarding career. So what's your choice?

CORPORATE STREETFIGHTER STRATEGY—BEING LIKED IS A NICETY; BEING RESPECTED IS A NECESSITY

As you move up the corporate ladder, being respected is much more important than being liked. Needing to be liked will be an obstacle to your career growth.

Lesson 1: Focus on Getting the Work Done

If you are the boss, getting the most productivity out of your team is essential. Do not try to be liked by everyone, as the concessions you make are unlikely to be appreciated but will most certainly impact your ability to be an effective leader in the company.

Lesson 2: Do Not Waste Your Precious Time Being Angry at Your Boss

It serves little purpose. As you have seen in earlier rounds, use that energy to figure out how to get what you want and advance your career. If you were passed over for a promotion, make the effort to learn what you need to do better.

DO YOU SEE YOURSELF AS AN EMPIRE BUILDER? SHOULD YOU?

We see them in every company—the people who think they should have it all and do it all. They feel that having more people reporting to them means they have more responsibility, and therefore, they are the most likely person to get promoted. However, they are missing some key points that could have a negative impact on their career.

More divisions and more people can result in less focus. Don't think for one minute that the higher-ups will be understanding when you don't deliver on something because you are overwhelmed by your responsibilities. They will just feel that you are not up to the task and that you already have too much on your plate. If the senior executives feel that way, it is unlikely your career will advance further.

Bosses are always happy when an executive subordinate says yes to taking on more and more responsibility. It is one less thing that they need to worry about when the company is acquiring other businesses or expanding product lines. They can always rely on good old (fill in *your name* here if this is you) to take on more work.

However, although they may be appreciative, they will *not* have your back when things go amiss. Referring back to round 3, I had the experience of being overwhelmed and blamed for many things. I allowed my boss to decrease my responsibilities, and that allowed me to get noticed for great performance and also improved my personal life dramatically.

So ask yourself: What do you think is more likely to get you to the next level? Having a lot of staff and responsibility but failing to deliver effectively or having fewer staff members and responsibility but getting noticed as an exceptional performer?

Another symptom of empire builders is they tend not to develop their team or hire the right people underneath them. After all there can only be one emperor in the empire. Of course, this just puts an added burden on them (see the next round on the martyr syndrome) and will eventually inhibit their ability to get promoted. As stated earlier it is important to have people in your division who can fill your shoes when you get promoted. Not having groomed such individuals is a failure that will be noticed by the executives in the company.

CORPORATE STREETFIGHTER STRATEGY—YOU DON'T NEED TO BUILD AN EMPIRE TO BE SUCCESSFUL, BUT YOU DO NEED TO BE SUCCESSFUL IN THE WORK YOU TAKE ON; TAKE ON ONLY AS MUCH WORK AS YOU CAN ACHIEVE WITH GREAT SUCCESS

Building an empire is not the best way to the top. As a matter of fact, it may hinder your progress. If you feel compelled to be an empire builder, hire and promote the best people you can find. These people will help you get to the top.

Lesson 1: Don't Build an Empire

Take on a reasonable amount of work and be great at what you do. It is better to be great with less than be mediocre with more. I only want the best performers. As a CEO I wanted all of my direct reports to be capable of taking my job, and I wanted my executives to hire the same way. In too many organiza-

> **It is better to be great with less than be mediocre with more.**

tions, there is an abyss in ability between the executive team and those who report to them.

Lesson 2: It Is OK to Say No

If you are working nonstop, have no personal life, and are struggling to keep your head above water, you can tell your boss your plate is full. Even if the boss puts pressure on you, you need to stick to your guns.

When you are overwhelmed and perform poorly, you will naturally expect some empathy. After all you only took on the extra work to please the boss. But it is all about performance, and if you are not performing well, you will get more pressure, resulting in more stress and even poorer performance, and it will have a detrimental effect on your personal life.

Lesson 3: It Is OK to Transfer Divisions to Others

After learning this lesson earlier in my career, I have given up more divisions and personnel than anyone else I know. I did not wait for someone to ask me. I generally would volunteer to give someone else an opportunity for personal and career growth by giving them some of my responsibilities (assuming they were ready to take them on).

To be completely honest, I had no aspirations to be a CEO when doing this. In general, I was looking to have a better life for myself while helping others have better career opportunities. But it did allow me to excel in the areas I remained in and ultimately resulted in my getting several executive roles that I do not think I would have gotten had I not made the decision to divest.

I am the only one that can handle this!

ARE YOU A MARTYR?

I have seen what I would call the martyr syndrome many times. This is often a person who has been with the company for a long time. Earlier in their career, they were promoted to a middle management position, and they have been stagnant in that position. They truly believe that the company will fall apart without them. Every time there is a crisis, they come riding in on their white horse to save the day.

The martyr is a hard worker and often will work nights and weekends to ensure that the company survives all crises. They make sure that everyone knows that they are doing so and what a disaster it would have been had they not taken charge themselves. Martyrs do most things themselves, as no one around them can be trusted to do it, and subconsciously, they need to get all the credit for "saving the day." They are appreciated by their peers and subordinates, as they carry a load that is much greater than most, and they always step up when there is a problem. But they clearly have not received the appreciation of upper management, as they have not been promoted in many years.

Does this sound like you? Are you consumed with the knowledge that the company could not survive without you, even though you have remained in a middle management position for a long time? Do you spend an inordinate amount of time at work and throw yourself into every crisis and wonder why (perhaps outside of a spot bonus every now and then) you haven't been promoted into a position of greater responsibility? Or have you convinced yourself that you should not be promoted as if you left your current position, you would be irreplaceable, and the harm to the company would be catastrophic?

The answer to the *why* is quite simple. Martyrdom has little to no place in the organization. Having a single person who does everything poses a substantial risk to the company, and the company would be far better off if you trained your team to do what you do. Yes, I know they won't be as good as you, but there will be good coverage for any issues that arise.

You can then spend your time mentoring and guiding the employees in your department, which will result in a network of people who can assist when there are issues. Then you really will be an asset to the company and likely get that elusive promotion and raise that never seems to happen despite your "heroic" efforts. You will get the rewards for your work while enjoying a much better personal life, and that is truly something to aspire to.

What if your CEO or other C-suite executives are martyrs? At that level we call it egotism or narcissism. The belief that only they can solve any and all problems will result in them becoming a funnel. This might work in a small company but not in a larger one, and it certainly will result in a lack of professional growth for those who report to them.

The best executive is the one who has sense enough to pick good men to do what he wants done, and self-restraint to keep from meddling with them while they do it.

—THEODORE ROOSEVELT

CORPORATE STREETFIGHTER STRATEGY— INVEST IN YOUR TEAM AND MAKE SURE THAT YOU ARE GROOMING A SUCCESSOR

As expressed in other rounds, if you have not groomed your team and a successor, then you have not done your job as a manager or leader. It is that simple. Martyrs may save a client or defuse a difficult situation, but in the end, they are dangerous. Martyrs are both a funnel that slows things down and a risk to the company because they have not shared their knowledge. They believe this gives them job security and ensures that they are needed, but in many cases, the company would be better off replacing them with a group of well-trained people.

Lesson 1: Do You Fit the Description of a Martyr? Assess Yourself

If the answer is yes, there is no time like the present to make a change. By adjusting your approach, you will find that you will move up the corporate ladder faster.

Lesson 2: Invest in Your Team

If you fit the martyr profile, rechannel your energy to being a productive driver of your group versus investing your energy in being a superman or a superwoman. You will work less hard, you will be able to share the load, you will improve your personal life, and you will be much more likely to advance your career.

Lesson 3: Do Not Assume That You Are Indispensable If You Are a Martyr

No one is indispensable. Many times when martyrs leave an organization, they check back to see how the place has fallen apart without them, only to learn the company is doing just fine. Don't hurt your career and, more importantly, miss out on family time to show how important you are. Trust that your knowledge is very useful and needs to be shared. A corporate streetfighter is strong as an individual but even stronger when using their skills to motivate an entire team or organization.

MISSING PERSON

A Competent, Creative, Intelligent Version of You

ROUND 21

DO YOU HAVE IMPOSTOR SYNDROME? NEVER UNDERESTIMATE YOURSELF

I have met with countless people who do not believe they can accomplish the goals they aspire to. Many feel they have been lucky to achieve what they have to date. Some of these people have what has been called impostor syndrome.

Impostor syndrome, also known as perceived fraudulence, involves feelings of self-doubt and personal incompetence that persist despite a person's education, experience, and accomplishments. Those suffering from this syndrome often end up working harder and holding themselves to higher standards than their peers but still feel undeserving of promotions and accolades. This syndrome disproportionately impacts people from marginalized identity groups and is not just about self-confidence. People with impostor syndrome can feel underserving because they have been treated differently or as less than their peers in a negative manner both inside and outside of workplace settings.

We have all heard of actors who state that they feel that their next movie may be their last and that they wonder when the shoe will drop and people will realize that they are not as good as their reputation. We often scratch our heads at this insecurity, as these people have made millions and millions of dollars practicing their craft, and we find it hard to believe that they can be so insecure. We also see this behavior in business situations, but it gets little attention. The people who get the most attention are the egotists and narcissists who are excellent at self-promotion and who may greatly exaggerate their abilities, but their confidence is so great that the perception of the masses is that a lot of what they say must be true.

Early in my career, an executive made a speech at one of our town hall meetings that really stuck with me. He said, "Never underestimate what you can personally do or accomplish if you put your mind and energy to work." It was an excellent speech but one that I had trouble buying into as a matter of experience. As a student and then a physician, I certainly knew this to be true, but my experience in the corporate environment had been mixed.

In one of my prior jobs, I had observed things moving very slowly. To get things done, you needed many approvals, which took a great deal of time. However, at another company, things were nimble, and individual contributors were recognized and allowed to pursue projects that would be personally rewarding and make the company better.

A corporate streetfighter knows their value and is proud of their achievements.

So the speech certainly was consistent with the culture of that organization.

The recognition of personal achievement and the coaching that led to the belief that we could all make a difference kept the prevalence of impostor syndrome to a minimum. Do not look to minimize the importance of your accomplishments. Do not attribute your success to luck. A corporate streetfighter knows their value and is proud of their achievements.

CORPORATE STREETFIGHTER STRATEGY— DON'T UNDERESTIMATE YOUR ACCOMPLISHMENTS AND ACHIEVEMENTS

It is important to realize that you have something to contribute and that you are capable of making a difference. You will come across plenty of self-promoters who will take advantage of your lack of confidence to get the promotions and raises that you are entitled to.

Lesson 1: Corporate Streetfighters Do Not Have Impostor Syndrome

Be self-reflective and see if you are suffering from impostor syndrome. Don't underestimate what you can accomplish for yourself and in your career. Think big and deliver for yourself. If you have any doubts, put together a list of your accomplishments so you can see your abilities in action.

Lesson 2: Wake up and Give Yourself the Credit You Deserve

Odds are that you deserve everything that you have achieved and that your accomplishments are no fluke. You certainly are doing yourself no favor in thinking of yourself as an impostor. Quite the opposite: You are missing out on opportunities that can be life changing.

Lesson 3: Changing Is Not Easy

I would love to say that the best way to fix this is to just not feel that way. But that is like saying don't be depressed because you shouldn't feel that way. The reality is that these behaviors are ingrained, and it will take work on your end, plus the help of a good coach, to see your situation in a different way.

Grow this way.

I HAVE GOOD, NEW IDEAS—BUT NO ONE IS LISTENING

The existence of any method, standard, custom, or practice is no reason for its continuance when a better is offered.

—THEODORE ROOSEVELT

Good, new ideas are not as common as you might think. When looking to implement change, the expression "We have always done it that way" as an excuse for not thinking has been particularly exasperating to me. When someone came to me with an idea, I always gauged their passion to proceed. If they accepted no for an answer, I felt that they really weren't all in, in their belief in their own idea.

I want people to fight for what they believe in, and that fight should be based on facts and not opinions. After all most executives will feel that their opinion is better than yours in the absence of facts. Prepare well for meetings where you are hoping to change things. Make sure you have considered all of the positives as well as the potential objections that you can think of before pitching the idea to your boss. You may not get a second chance.

If there is a difference of opinion between you and your boss in regard to your idea, trying to prove your boss wrong will most assuredly backfire. The higher the score your boss got when you did the assessment in round 3, the more likely it is that your boss will not react kindly to you trying to show that you are smarter than they are.

The advice I give in these situations is, "Do you want to prove you are right, or do you want to win?" Some may say, "What's the difference?" Well, if you prove you are right, then your boss will be wrong. If you have read this far into the book, you know that probably isn't going to end well for you. You might say, "But if I win, doesn't that mean the boss lost?" The key to that question is why playing to win is so important.

If you really have a great idea and the boss lets you proceed and it is successful, you both win. You get to pursue something you are passionate about, and the boss has a success in the department that will help their career. Hopefully, even if just acting in their own best interests, they now realize your value and should want to bring you up the corporate ladder with them to supply them with more ideas.

CORPORATE STREETFIGHTER STRATEGY—THINK BIG AND BE READY TO EXECUTE YOUR IDEAS

You do not have to be a Steve Jobs or a Bill Gates with world-changing ideas; you just need to be the best version of yourself. The impact of your ideas can be large or small, but the important thing is that they will be meaningful to the business and give you the pride of knowing that you made it happen.

Lesson 1: If You Have an Idea, Speak Up

I believe that most people have had at least one idea that would have made them wealthy had they acted upon it. How many times have you or someone you know said, "I had that idea," when they hear of someone making millions of dollars with something new?

Lesson 2: Exceptional Ideas Are Rare

All of your ideas may not be great. They may contribute to a company's success, or they may not be worth considering. The important thing is that you advocate for your ideas as corporate streetfighters and do not take no without a fight. When your ideas are not considered worthy of pursuing, you need to learn *why* for personal growth.

Lesson 3: Implementation of Your Idea Is Extremely Important

Coming up with ideas is an important skill, but it is essential that those ideas can be implemented at a reasonable cost and on a reasonable timeline. If you want to receive the maximum reward for your idea, you need to make it happen. Don't underestimate what you can accomplish for yourself and in your career. Think big and deliver for yourself.

ROUND 23

BE DECISIVE WITHOUT FEAR OF FAILURE OR CRITICISM

In any moment of decision, the best thing you can do is the right thing. The worst thing you can do is nothing.

—THEODORE ROOSEVELT

Instead of spending our lives running towards our dreams, we are often running away from a fear of failure or a fear of criticism.

—ERIC WRIGHT

In round 4 I discussed my 360° evaluation. One question was: When faced with a difficult decision, should you use the information at hand to make a prompt decision, or should you take some time and analyze the situation? I answered that I would take time to analyze the situation, and I was told that I was too analytical, which is not uncommon for physicians.

I then asked if it was a trick question and if either answer could be right or wrong in order to drive a discussion. I was informed that at an executive level, decisiveness is more important than analysis.

At an executive level, decisiveness is more important than analysis.

This was something I did not really agree with at the time, but later I became a firm believer. In my role as a corporate executive, I have consistently forgiven errors of commission but not errors of omission. It is very important to me that people act!

How many times have you gone to your boss with a problem that they did not address or did not address promptly? How many times have you sat in meetings where everyone tried to show how smart they were, but no actions were taken? How many times has your boss been unsure of the right thing to do, so the resultant procrastination left you holding the bag, with customers or coworkers taking the heat while the boss remained in the background?

If any or all of these things have happened to you, you already know the importance of making a decision. When people ask me how I know my decisions are right, I tell them that it is more important for me to make the decision than to be right all of the time. I tell them, "I hope that I am right at least 51 percent of the time!" Most decisions would not break the back of the organization if the action taken is not 100 percent correct, but constant analysis without decision-making can indeed destroy an organization. I have seen this happen too many times both at the divisional and corporate levels when insecure leadership results in a lack of action.

So why don't people make decisions? Fear of making a mistake, fear of criticism, fear of failure, and fear of blame are the most likely reasons. Let's look at each of these common areas of concern.

FEAR OF MAKING A MISTAKE

The only man who never makes a mistake is the one who never does anything.

—THEODORE ROOSEVELT

I was meeting with a senior executive in the middle of a crisis with a client. Action was needed, and little was being done. The executive relayed to me that he was unsure of what to do and that he did not feel comfortable giving a response to the client. I decided to press the issue, and the conversation went something like this.

> **ME:** Have you responded to the client? It's been over twenty-four hours since they contacted us.

> **EXECUTIVE:** I decided to let the project manager handle this, and I have been assisting by gathering documentation.

> **ME:** As the executive I would suggest that you call and tell them that you are conducting a thorough investigation, and make sure you give them a firm date in the near future when you will contact them again.

EXECUTIVE: Getting this communication wrong can cost us this deal and our relationship with the client. I don't want to make a mistake, so I want to wait until I am sure of what I am communicating.

ME: Not responding will assuredly cost us this deal and our relationship with the client.

EXECUTIVE: Can we make a pact? You help me here so I don't make a mistake, and I will help you not make mistakes either.

ME: I am sure I make mistakes every day, and I do not worry about making them. What I do worry about is inaction. I will help you by calling the client myself and explaining the situation.

Several months later I asked this executive to leave our company. Every decision came down to the risk of making a mistake, and both his team and I were frustrated. In a theme that tends to repeat itself, the thing the executive most feared was losing their job, and they had just done so. This happened because being afraid of making a mistake was the biggest *mistake* they could have made.

FEAR OF CRITICISM

It is not the critic who counts: not the man who points out how the strong man stumbles or where the doer of deeds could have done them better. The credit belongs to the man who is actually in the arena, whose face is marred by dust and sweat and blood, who strives valiantly, who errs and comes up short again and again ... who, at the best, knows, in the end, the triumph of high achievement, and who, at the worst, if he fails, at least he fails while daring greatly.

—THEODORE ROOSEVELT

To escape criticism, do nothing, say nothing, be nothing.

—ELBERT HUBBARD

If you fear criticism, it is just the other side of the coin of fearing to make a mistake. So someone may criticize your decisions; so what? The role of the critic, whether it be your boss or a colleague, is the easy one. The hard role is coming up with something to do, and the more creative and innovative the idea, the more likely you are to be criticized.

Whenever someone who works for me comes up with an idea that I criticize, I always follow with "I have the easy job of listening and criticizing, but it is rare to have someone who comes up with ideas." I then go on to tell them what I like and don't like about their suggestions and encourage them to keep working on their idea. I want them to come back to me with a more fully formed idea that includes implementation. If they can do that in a convincing manner, I let them proceed with implementing it even if I disagree, provided that I believe it will not have a serious negative impact on the company if things go wrong. But before I do, I always ask for the following agreement.

"If you see things going wrong, please do not persist just to try to prove yourself right and me wrong, as that will not end well for you. However, if it is a great success, gloating is allowed, so feel free to come to my office and crow about your great success. Nothing would make me happier than to have you prove me wrong!"

I realize that very few bosses have the same opinion on this that I do. I have been frustrated many times, as my ideas have been ignored in the interest of playing it safe and doing things the way they have always been done. At an early point in my career, I had a conversation with my senior executive boss that went something like this:

BOSS: Why are you so intent on doing anything that rocks the boat here?

ME: I came here to make a difference.

BOSS: We have a way of doing things around here, and any deviation can lead to criticism, and we could lose our jobs.

ME: Wouldn't you agree that the way things are done can be improved?

BOSS: Yes, but the most important thing is to just keep things the way they are. Don't you want to keep earning a good salary with bonuses and stock options?

ME: You retired into this job, but I actually want to accomplish something in my life and career. There is so much opportunity to improve things, and it seems that people are receptive.

BOSS: Yes, people are receptive to improving things, but you will get little support to change things. In the end that will likely result in failure, and you will lose your job. More importantly, it will reflect badly on me, so I don't want you to do anything like that.

As discussed in round 14, several months later a colleague of mine had a great idea that he wanted to try. Our boss said no, so he went over the boss's head and got approval. There were many people who thought it would benefit the company. He asked for my assistance, and I gave it. And it was a great success. Our boss got credit for our work and got a large bonus and stock award, but our boss was angry with us for doing it, and we did not get any financial benefit. However, we did get admonished for doing something that he did not want us to do!

Was this project a success or a failure? It is something for you to think about. What is your answer? As for my colleague and myself, within six months we had both left the organization and went on to have very successful careers.

FEAR OF BLAME

Do what you feel in your heart to be right—for you'll be criticized anyway. You'll be damned if you do, and damned if you don't.

—ELEANOR ROOSEVELT

I am not a believer in blame, period. There is nothing useful that can be accomplished by blaming people when things go wrong, especially since often the person pointing fingers and doing the blaming is the person who had a good deal to do with the problem in the first place. They would best be guided by this quote:

If you could kick the person in the pants responsible for most of your trouble, you wouldn't sit for a month.

—THEODORE ROOSEVELT

Unfortunately, there are many offices where blame is a routine part of life. One such example was my recollection of a conversation I had with a CEO concerning an employee who always seemed to be the subject of the CEO's wrath. I had just taken a leadership role in this division a few weeks earlier to solve the issues discussed below:

CEO: You need to fire Employee X, as he is responsible for the poor quality, cost overruns, and delays of our new system. He is not managing our vendor properly.

ME: Why are you always picking on Employee X? I think he is doing a good job, and I work with him every day. Also, there was a whole team of people working on the new system. Why is he the subject of your wrath and not the head of the department or the other people involved?

CEO: He wanted a promotion to be in charge of data, we put him in charge of data, and therefore, he is responsible for the new system.

ME: You have a whole division that does nothing but build software, and you have not involved them at all with this project. Instead, you choose to blame someone in charge of data who knows nothing about building new software systems.

CEO: Well then, he should not have taken the job.

ME: What job? He has no idea that you think he is in charge of this project. Did you ever specifically tell him he is in charge?

CEO: No, that is something he should have understood when he took his new position.

ME: You mean the new position that has nothing to do with software development.

CEO: Well, we disagree on that.

ME: Yes, we do. I think if you really want to know who to blame, you should go home and take a look in the mirror. This project has been delayed for months at a significant cost to our company, and you never even asked a question about the vendor we are using or how the project is going. Now you wake up when the project is due and decide that the best cause of action is to blame someone and fire them. Well, that is not happening.

I did a complete investigation, and as it turned out, there were many people responsible for the problems with this project. One major culprit was the vendor we had hired to do the work. I ended up firing the vendor and bringing the project in-house to be developed by our internal team. They did a great job, and the new system was a great success. And the employee the CEO wanted me to fire enjoyed a long and successful career with the company.

I want to make it clear that although I don't believe in blame, I am a big believer in accountability. I once had a boss who did not understand the difference. He was blaming someone, and I said that I would certainly hold them accountable. He said that is the same as blaming them. I tried to explain that holding someone accountable was necessary for good business and that it would be a chance for learning and self-improvement, but blame was negative from a work and emotional standpoint. He then replied that he really didn't see the difference!

You must be accountable for any work or any projects you take on. That means taking responsibility for the work and outcome as well as the work of the people working with you on the project. My rule of thumb in speaking with employees has always been "I don't care if you are 95 percent responsible for the project, and a coworker is 5 percent responsible for the project. As far as I am concerned, *you are both accountable* for the result."

By removing blame from the picture and holding everyone involved accountable, there are fewer failures and certainly fewer surprises.

Some may say that is unfair, but the point of it is if the person who is 5 percent accountable sees things going wrong, they will now let me know as opposed to the usual occurrence of just letting the person who is 95 percent responsible take the blame when things go wrong. By removing blame from the picture and holding everyone involved accountable, there are fewer failures and certainly fewer surprises.

FEAR OF FAILURE

It is hard to fail, but it is worse never to have tried to succeed.

—THEODORE ROOSEVELT

It has always been my opinion that living in fear of failure is almost a guarantee that you will never succeed at any major task. It is a self-fulfilling prophecy. A corporate streetfighter should fight to win, not worry about what might happen if things go wrong.

Things always go wrong, but if you are well prepared and have a winning attitude, you can overcome these issues and still be successful. Failure for someone who lives in fear of failure just reaffirms their fears and will reinforce their belief that they should remain below the radar and not risk doing something that could be a game changer.

If at first you don't succeed, try, try again.

—THOMAS H. PALMER

There was a point early in my business career when I took a few jobs that would have been considered high risk, high reward, and they did not work out as I had hoped. Taking a calculated risk is in my nature, and I have always been willing to bet on myself. These failures, although not catastrophic, were certainly discouraging. However, I am a student of history, and watching documentaries about some very successful people, I learned the following:

- Milton Hershey failed twice before coming up with a successful candy business.

- R. H. Macy had at least four store failures before he found success.

- Walt Disney's first animation company went bankrupt. He created a very successful cartoon character (Oswald the Rabbit), only to find that his animators and the rights to the character had been co-opted by his producer. Rather than give up, he went on to create Mickey Mouse, and the rest is history.

Although I always worked hard and I was good at my jobs, that generally was not enough, as we all need a little bit (or a lot) of luck. Finally, due to persistence, I found myself in the right job, in the right place, at the right time. In the end perseverance and determination won the day.

CORPORATE STREETFIGHTER STRATEGY—DON'T BE AFRAID TO FAIL AND LEARN FROM IT

The most successful people will tell you that fear is inversely proportional to success. A corporate streetfighter must overcome fears of mistakes, criticism, blame, and failure to achieve success. Working with a mentor or coach can help you if you are struggling with your fears.

Lesson 1: We All Make Mistakes

Fear of making mistakes in your work life or personal life just leads to not trying the things that could change your life. Mistakes are part of our growth. I never learned anything from getting something right, as it could have been luck versus great thinking, but I have learned a lot from my mistakes. Most important of which was not to repeat them!

Lesson 2: Criticizing Someone Else Is Easy; Coming Up with Ideas and Strategies Is Hard

Don't let the critics discourage you. There are a lot of famous actors, athletes, authors, et al. who were told that they had no chance to be successful but went on to have brilliant careers. Keep trying!

Lesson 3: There Is No Room for Blame, *Period*

Blame is all about negativity. It makes the person who was blamed and those around them fearful and less likely to make contributions to the business.

Lesson 4: Failure Is a Part of Work and Life, and You Need to Learn from Your Failures

If you learn from your failures, they become more like lessons and less like failures. Some are extremely tough lessons, but the point is that you must learn from them. These lessons will come in handy when you are faced with difficult situations in the future, and you have been there and done that.

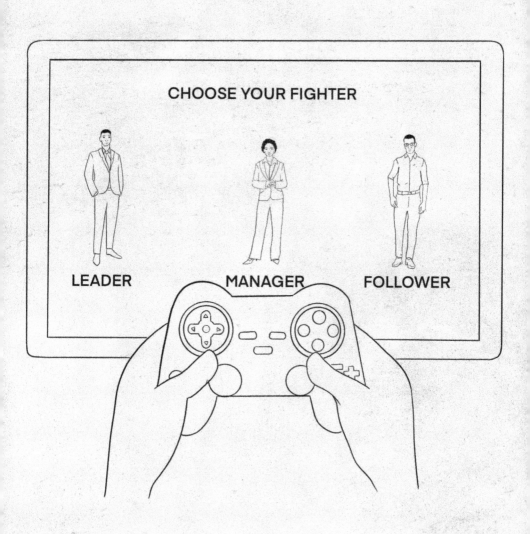

ARE YOU A LEADER, FOLLOWER, OR MANAGER?

People ask the difference between a leader and a boss ... The leader works in the open, and the boss in covert. The leader leads, and the boss drives.

—THEODORE ROOSEVELT

ARE YOU A LEADER?

There are many different types of leaders. But being a leader does not guarantee a good result.

Are you a leader like General Custer? He was a poor student at West Point. As a matter of fact, he was last in his class and wasn't much for discipline or following rules. His leadership style was inspirational, as he led his troops from the front as opposed to generals who stayed behind the lines. His leadership resulted in a confident group that won several important battles during the Civil War. But ultimately, his huge ego and feeling of being invincible led to his demise and the demise of his troops at Little Bighorn. Just like General Custer, an inspirational leader can lead their business to ruin as well as success.

Are you a leader like Madam C. J. Walker? She was the first American woman, let alone an African American woman, to become a self-made millionaire. The first in her family to be born free, she was orphaned at age seven, married at age fourteen, and widowed at age twenty. As a single mother earning $1.50 a day as a washerwoman, she had little hope of having a successful life and career. When she started suffering from hair loss, she developed a hair product for herself that was appealing to other African American women. When others wouldn't invest in her business, she reinvested her own money into other cosmetic products and built a business empire. Just like Madam C. J. Walker, you do not have to have started in this world with many advantages if you have a great idea and are willing to act on it.

> **You do not have to have started in this world with many advantages if you have a great idea and are willing to act on it.**

Are you a leader like George Washington? He made several mistakes in his younger years, and his actions contributed to the start of the French and Indian War. But Washington learned from his mistakes. He was respected by all, and during the American Revolution, he kept his troops together despite a lack of support from Congress, lack of food, and poor shelter. He was a great statesman and probably could have installed himself with almost kinglike powers but instead chose to do what he felt best for the new republic of the United States. Just like George Washington, an early mistake that you learn from does not have to be the end of your career. Your mistakes should lead to wisdom, and when paired with leadership and political astuteness, you can earn the respect of many and go on to do great things.

Do you fit the description of one of the people above? If so, which of the above are you? Do you have a little of each of them, or are you nothing like them? They were all leaders, but they also had to overcome adversity. Clearly, you do not have to be perfect to be a leader, but you should recognize the behaviors that will hold you back from achieving greater success.

Some people are born to lead and others to follow. Some are great at managing processes but not people. Some are great at getting the work done but not at inspiring the team to new heights. What are your qualities? The best executives are leaders who encourage and inspire their teams to do more than most of them thought possible and in getting to that achievement, opening their eyes to what is possible and what more can be done.

For those readers with C-suite aspirations, leadership of this kind will not only help get you to the top but will also make you successful. Most of you know who the leaders are. They are the ones you look up to and want to follow. Leaders may not be the best managers or the best at driving results, but they make you want to achieve the results.

If a leader does not have metric-driven operational skills, it is best if they pair up with someone who does. But that can only be done if the leader is not an egotist or narcissist who thinks they are the best at everything. In that case the leader may inspire you at the start, but over time it will be shown that the company is not delivering on the promise it has and that although the boss may inspire you, the company is not achieving its goals.

ARE YOU A FOLLOWER?

There is nothing wrong with being a follower, but it is important to know that is what you are. If you are happy to have someone else take the lead for getting things done while you do your part, or you are always looking for someone else to come up with the solution to a problem, then you are a follower.

If you are a follower, it is very important that you support your boss in what they do (see round 8), as they will appreciate that they can count on you when needed, and if they are a bit insecure, you will not be viewed as a threat, and you should be treated well. If you are a follower, you will probably never make it to the C-suite of a large company, but you can still end up with a management position, as your boss may bring you up as they move up, as they know you can be counted on. You may also be quite adept at running a small business on your own. It is important to note that most people fall in this category, and companies could not function without them.

ARE YOU A MANAGER?

Managers can be people with leadership potential, or they can be followers. The most important thing is for you to know what description best suits you and what your strengths and weaknesses are. Managers can be good at managing processes, people, or both. In my career I have preferred to have great employees manage a process versus a great process being managed by average employees, but I have seen several successful executives who focus on the process, and the people just need to follow along.

Whatever your style is, as a manager you need to manage to get things done! In round 17 I reviewed the skill sets that I feel are necessary to be a manager, director, vice president, or member of the

C-suite. But in this round, I am asking you to look into the core of who you are as a person. The best path to success is to know yourself and to address and/or compensate for your weaknesses while displaying your strengths.

CORPORATE STREETFIGHTER STRATEGY— KNOW YOUR SKILL SETS AND HOW THEY CAN POSITION YOU FOR SUCCESS IN YOUR CAREER

We are all wired differently and are blessed with different skill sets. It is important to know where you stand as a leader in order to determine your destiny as a corporate executive. One can argue whether leaders are born or made, but what is clear is that most people recognize who the leaders in an organization are. Corporate streetfighters should be at the top of the list.

Lesson 1: Assess Your Abilities and Skill Set

You are well served if you do an honest self-assessment. Are you a leader, a follower, or a manager? If you have C-suite aspirations, you will need to be a leader.

Lesson 2: Contemplate Your Future Career Goals

Does your personality and skill set match that aspiration? If not, self-reflection and coaching can help open your eyes to where you need to change.

Lesson 3: Be the Best Version of Yourself

No matter what category you are in, it is important to be comfortable with yourself and make the best of what you have to offer.

NO GUTS, NO GLORY— TAKING SUCCESS TO THE NEXT LEVEL

Do you want a walk on part in the war or the lead role in a cage?

—PINK FLOYD

How many times have you heard someone say that they were smarter or just as smart as the founder of a business, that they had the same idea, and that they could've been rich or done it better? Perhaps you have harbored the same thoughts.

I feel that everyone has had at least one idea in their life that would have made them wealthy and changed their lives, but they did not act. Why didn't they act? It could have been many reasons. Perhaps they really didn't believe as much in the idea as they now say they do, having seen it has become successful. They had no idea how to get the idea implemented. They didn't have the money to start a business. Or perhaps they were just afraid of the risk. All of these are legitimate reasons for inaction, but they are also the things that separate the entrepreneur from the pack. Entrepreneurs tend to pursue their ideas regardless of the risk because they believe in their idea and in their ability to make it happen.

Whatever you do, you need courage. Whatever course you decide upon, there is always someone to tell you that you are wrong. There are always difficulties arising that tempt you to believe your critics are right.

—RALPH WALDO EMERSON

Several years ago I gave a talk to a large group of pharmaceutical company scientists. In my consulting role, I had come across several examples where studies were, in my opinion, done unnecessarily, as the scientist should have been able to predict the outcome based on the preclinical information available to them. So I asked the group why they did not have the courage to speak up and notify their superiors that the study was going to fail. The answer was that their bosses wanted the study done. I then repeated my question. "If you already knew the outcome, why waste precious time and resources on doing a study that was not going to succeed?"

One lone person raised his hand and said, "I was worried I would be fired if I disagreed with what my superiors wanted to do."

I replied, "That is what I mean by courage!" Then a large, sheepish sound of laughter took over the room. Perhaps the individual was right, or maybe he actually would have been rewarded for saving the company time and effort in a fruitless task. In any event, once proven right, regardless of the initial response he might have received,

I would think that his credibility in the future would have been greatly enhanced.

IF YOU ARE OFFERED A PROMOTION AND YOU ARE NOT SURE YOU CAN DO THE JOB, SHOULD YOU TAKE IT?

Whenever you are asked if you can do a job, tell 'em, "Certainly I can!" Then get busy and find out how to do it.

—THEODORE ROOSEVELT

The majority of my career has been driven by my ability to recognize opportunities when they arose and to take advantage of them. This worked out for me, but as I pointed out earlier, having a plan is much better!

I have been fearless in stepping into jobs that a more cautious person may have avoided, as I always had a strong belief in myself, my ability to work with others, and my ability to learn quickly. If I was confident that I had the skill set, I was willing to step up and take the job. And as a fan of Theodore Roosevelt, I followed his advice above to a *T*!

The ability to have more control was a driving factor throughout my career, and although money was a consideration, I never took a job or a promotion for the money. The first time the opportunity came for me to throw my hat into the ring to become a CEO, I declined. Having run operations for many years and having implemented most of my ideas, I was happy to have someone else in the role. Achieving the title of CEO was not an aspiration of mine, and I was not sure how well suited I would be to the role.

Watching the TV show *Undercover Boss* increased my courage to step up and apply for the CEO job the next time there was an opportunity. Many of the CEOs on that show knew very little of what was really going on in their companies, and they were still CEOs. I knew almost everything that was going on in my company. Also, things had evolved in the business where I felt my skill set was now the most appropriate for the role. I got the job!

Even with a strong belief in yourself, if you don't truly have the skill set needed, you can be on the road to a major failure. In a somewhat humorous family example, my grandfather came to this country in his teens, and he was trained as a tailor. After a few years in New York City, he hopped on a train to explore the Western United States and worked as a tailor in the Pacific Northwest before ending up in postearthquake San Francisco. There he got a job with a high-quality tailor shop by essentially telling the owner that he could do anything and everything that was required of him. Unfortunately, that ended up with my grandfather being chased out of the shop, as his boss tried to stab him with a pair of scissors. But fortunately, that led to his return to the East Coast, where he met my grandmother, which eventually led to me!

Stick to your guns if you are asked to take on more responsibility than you are comfortable with.

It is important to stick to your guns if you are asked to take on more responsibility than you are comfortable with. My boss once came to me and said he wanted to promote someone who was an executive with little operating experience to be a general manager of a large division of our company. I thought this person had a lot of skills and could someday be a good operator, but he would need a lot of coaching to start an operating career at the top. That being said, I would have supported this, as we needed someone who was smart and trustworthy, and I felt that he could learn the role with help.

The executive turned the opportunity down, and my boss was beside himself. The boss felt he was offering this executive the opportunity of a lifetime. The boss then asked me to speak with this executive in order to change his mind. The executive had clearly thought it through very carefully before deciding that the job just wasn't right for him. He outlined all the ways that failure was possible and that, even with support, it could be a struggle that wasn't worth the risk.

It was a very cogent argument against taking the job, and after hearing his presentation, I agreed he should not take the job. Well, later that day, my boss came in to tell me how I was not helping him and that he instructed me to convince this person to take the job and not to agree that the job was too big. I explained that it was my intention to convince the executive to take the job, but it was clear that there was great discomfort and fear of failure. That convinced me that the person would not be successful, despite my personal belief that he could do the job.

CORPORATE STREETFIGHTER STRATEGY—KNOW WHETHER YOU ARE WILLING TO TAKE RISKS OR PREFER A MORE CONSERVATIVE APPROACH

It is wrong to push someone into a situation that they believe will have a negative outcome both personally and professionally. Neither my boss nor I would have turned an opportunity like this down, as it is our nature to seek the next challenge. That mindset helped make us the leaders of companies, but not everyone is wired that way.

A person's appetite for risk and degree of confidence in their ability play a huge role in what they can accomplish. You don't need to take career risks to be a corporate streetfighter, but at some point, you will need to be confident enough to move forward.

Lesson 1: Weigh the Risk versus the Benefit When Opportunity Knocks

We all know the names of groundbreaking entrepreneurs like Bill Gates, Steve Jobs, and Jeff Bezos who could have taken an easy path with modest success but instead tried something new and reached astronomical heights. Of course, there are probably one hundred stories of failure and/or mediocre results for every story of super success. Risks need to be taken to blaze a new trail and achieve great success, but slow and steady is also OK as long as you keep moving forward in your career.

Lesson 2: If You Are Completely Risk Averse, Do Not Blame Others If You Do Not Achieve What You Had Hoped For

Very few people will become titans of industry, but there are lots of opportunities for life-changing moments by taking smaller, calculated risks. Know your own appetite for risk and act appropriately.

Extra Lesson

Try not to be in a position where someone is chasing you around the office, trying to stab you for a mistake you have made at work! Your children and grandchildren will thank you.

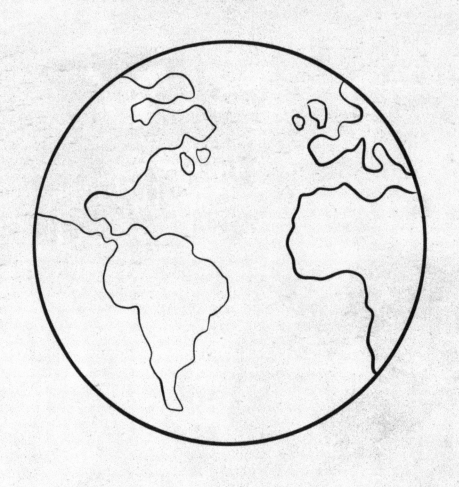

ROUND 26

INTERNATIONAL BUSINESS IS ALL ABOUT CULTURE

I was looking to outsource some cardiology work to India but only wanted to work with the highest-rated physicians available. The owner of a cardiology practice in India convinced me that he had the right team to do the job, that they were tech savvy enough to use our systems, and that they would provide the twenty-four-hour coverage we were seeking.

I spent a good deal of time and money training them, getting the technology set up, and testing them to make sure they were as good as any physicians we had in the United States and Europe. We got them up and running, and they hardly ever showed up to work! My team and I had to work late into the evening many times to cover for the work they should have been doing, and then I terminated the contract, vowing never to try that again.

A contractor of mine who had contacts in India said that I should not give up and that I should meet someone who he knew could put this together successfully. The person he introduced me to was a technology entrepreneur, not a physician, which made me very skeptical, but they both insisted they could get me even better cardiologists, and they were willing to guarantee performance. I reluctantly agreed, but this time it turned out to be a great success.

Always wanting to learn, I asked the entrepreneur why he was successful. He said, "Jeff, I know the culture in my country, and I understand how the cardiologists need to be treated to stay engaged." He went on to explain how he had chauffeurs waiting for the cardiologists after their day at the hospital, provided them with dinner on arriving to the office, had the chauffeurs wait and drive them home after work, and had 24/7 technology support available should the cardiologists have a technical issue when doing work from home. He explained that, although foreign to me, that is the minimum that should be done for cardiologists with their status in India.

I learned a lesson that has been invaluable to me as the companies I worked for acquired businesses in Europe and Japan. Americans often try to impose American culture on companies they own globally. But the people in those companies have a culture that is often very different from ours. This generally results in friction and failure. It is important to learn what motivates each employee to do their best work, and that can vary from country to country.

Learn what motivates each employee to do their best work, and that can vary from country to country.

I took great pride in earning the trust and respect of my international colleagues. I learned that the United States and the UK really can be two countries separated by a common language, not to mention the importance of teatime. In Germany and Japan, I took the time to learn that some of the things I said did not translate well and that some of the things I wanted to do to improve relations could have been perceived as insulting. Most importantly, I listened. I created an open environment that people in some cultures were not used to, and that took time and trust to develop but proved vital to my success. I was also able to dispel some feelings about American culture that I felt were stereotypical and were creating obstacles to the development of a true partnership.

CORPORATE STREETFIGHTER STRATEGY—MAKE SURE YOU TAKE CULTURAL DIFFERENCES INTO ACCOUNT

It is important to keep an open mind when working globally. Do not assume you know how to work and motivate people in different cultures and instead learn to be sensitive to the cultures you are working in. A corporate streetfighter is most inspired when they have good people in their corner who are helping them win.

Lesson 1: Understand the Culture of the Offices and the People You Work With

This can be true in the same company in the same country, but it is certainly true when working internationally. Just making the effort can often go a long way to establishing trust and cooperation.

Lesson 2: Apply Your Cultural Learnings to Your Management Style

It is not enough to try to learn about culture; you must use what you have learned to get the most out of your relationships. It is important that you are sincere in these efforts, as people will know if you are just going through the motions or if you are truly interested in what *they* are concerned about.

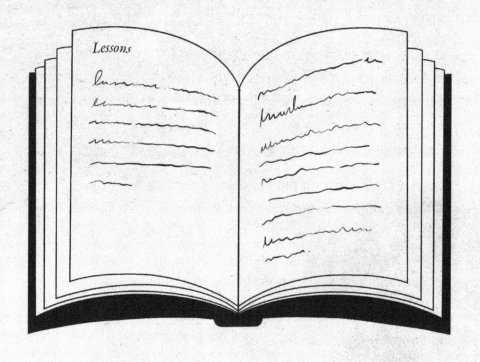

ROUND 27

JUST THE LESSONS

Of course, I hope you read both chapters and every round of this book, as I believe the context in which the lessons are presented is important, but for those of you who like an abbreviated version, I have listed all the lessons below in a quick form that is easy to review. This can be a useful tool of reference after you have read the book to quickly find the points of interest to you, and the round numbers are present to use as a quick reference.

I also want to invite you to visit my website:

www.corporatestreetfighter.com

for great updates and podcasts. I also select some of your questions to answer on my podcasts, so be sure to send them in!

CHAPTER 1

Round 1: What Kind of Boss Do You Have?

LESSON 1: Take stock of your current situation.

LESSON 2: Use the information, insights, and especially the lessons I provide for you to guide you to the best possible responses to the situation you are in.

Round 2: Realizing the Power of Managing Your Boss

LESSON 1: As a corporate streetfighter, you should always be prepared and play to win.

LESSON 2: Do not try to change your boss.

LESSON 3: Learn what gets your boss's attention and what does not.

Round 3: How the Worst Boss Forced Me to Develop the Skills for Success

LESSON 1: It is not enough to know you are doing a good job. It is just as important to present what you are doing in a manner that allows for that work to be recognized.

LESSON 2: Think carefully about the purpose of your work rather than just doing your work.

LESSON 3: Learning is a lifelong pursuit. Even the most difficult of bosses has something to teach you if you can separate your emotions from the interaction.

Round 4: Your Boss Is Not Omnipresent or Psychic

LESSON 1: It is up to you to drive the communication with your boss.

LESSON 2: When people take the time to mentor you, if the advice doesn't hit home at the time, don't just ignore it or say it doesn't apply to you. File it away for future reference and reflection.

Round 5: My Introduction to the Power of Knowing Your Boss

LESSON 1: Whether you like your boss or not, there is generally a reason they got to be where they are in the company. Listen to their advice, take criticism well, and then decide whether that advice suits you and your personality.

LESSON 2: Often it is the little things that can result in success or failure.

LESSON 3: You never know the benefit of your experiences at the time you have them.

Round 6: Your Boss Needs Your Support to Be Successful and Vice Versa

LESSON 1: If you work in a company with multiple offices, try to apply what you know about your office to the company as a whole. Corporate is unlikely to proceed with a plan that is different in every office.

LESSON 2: If communication is difficult with your boss, try to figure out how to change your approach, as you should not count on the boss changing their approach.

LESSON 3: When a decision is made, being subversive and/ or not giving 100 percent to the tasks assigned to you will not go unnoticed. It will hurt the company, your department, and your career.

LESSON 4: Failure, to a degree, is OK as long as lessons are learned.

Round 7: Arguing with the Boss—Win with Facts and Keep Emotions in Check

LESSON 1: Sometimes we let our emotions get the best of us. Try to keep your emotions in check and stick to the facts. It is hard to change your boss's mind, but your best bet is with facts and data, not emotions or opinions.

LESSON 2: Don't give your boss an opportunity to distract the discussion.

Round 8: Asking Your Boss for Greater Independence

LESSON 1: Ask to do more on your own, as you will learn very little just doing what is dictated to you by your boss.

LESSON 2: Do not try to change the world right out of the box. Do something with a very high probability of success.

Round 9: When Is a "Good" Boss Actually a "Bad" Boss?

LESSON 1: Having a boss who "protects" you or makes excuses for you is not good for your career. If you make a mistake, own it. We all make mistakes.

LESSON 2: Understand that if you are doing a good job, you deserve to be in that job, and that a boss who talks about you behind your back, excusing your performance, is not doing you any favors.

CHAPTER 2

Round 10: Have a Plan for Your Career

> **LESSON 1:** Play the long game as you look for your first or second career opportunity.
>
> **LESSON 2:** If you are interested in advancement and you are good at what you do, a fast-growth company is much more likely to provide opportunities for advancement.
>
> **LESSON 3:** If you are happy with your job/company and being promoted is more of a plus than a necessity, there is nothing wrong with staying and having a career with that company.
>
> **LESSON 4:** Be proactive. Have a plan for your own advancement, and do not rely on fate or opportunity rising up to meet you.
>
> **LESSON 5:** Once you have a plan, *act on it!*

Round 11: Making a Good First Impression and Negotiating a Salary When Starting a New Job

> **LESSON 1:** Come *prepared* to an interview. It is embarrassing to come to an interview and know nothing about the company.
>
> **LESSON 2:** Use each interview to advance your knowledge of the job and the company.
>
> **LESSON 3:** Keep your answers concise, and let the interviewer speak. Generally, the more the interviewer speaks, the better they think the interview was.

LESSON 4: Interview to win the job, then discuss salary and benefits. First, get the offer, then look at the whole package including salary, bonus, and benefits. Never negotiate against yourself. Let them make the first move.

Round 12: Exposure to Executives after You Are Hired

LESSON 1: Have an elevator speech prepared. Make sure to put your best foot forward and make a good impression whenever you get exposure to senior executives.

LESSON 2: Talk about things that are important to the business and showcase yourself to senior executives when you have the opportunity.

LESSON 3: Perception is reality. Executives tend to remember interactions with people if they are impactful.

Round 13: Your First Job—How Long Should You Stay?

LESSON 1: The grass is not always greener elsewhere.

LESSON 2: Your knowledge is your job portability.

Round 14: If You Want the Promotion, Ask for It (Especially in Sales and Marketing)

LESSON 1: Show your interest in the position when it becomes available.

LESSON 2: If you feel you are deserving of advancement and a suitable position is available, ask for the job.

LESSON 3: If you keep getting passed over for promotions, some self-assessment is in order. Have a frank discussion with your boss as to what you may be missing or lacking and how they would rate your performance.

LESSON 4: Don't make getting a promotion a condition of getting the work done.

Round 15: Asking for a Raise or a Bonus

LESSON 1: Many bosses are not good about verbally acknowledging people's work, let alone providing a financial reward for what is done. Speak up if you feel your accomplishments are not recognized.

LESSON 2: Don't let yourself or your work be taken for granted.

LESSON 3: Don't threaten to quit without another acceptable offer in hand. You may find yourself out of a job.

LESSON 4: If you are looking to leave the company for lack of raises or promotions, be sure that is the real and perhaps the only reason you want to leave.

Round 16: Stages of Career Advancement

LESSON 1: Understand what it takes to hold a certain role in a company.

LESSON 2: Assess your skill set to truly see if you belong in that role based upon your current capabilities.

Round 17: Your First Promotion

LESSON 1: Your first promotion can be the hardest. Go into the role with your eyes open.

LESSON 2: If your boss is a mentor, be thankful and learn as much as you can from them.

LESSON 3: Treat each employee as an individual. Find out what motivates them and how to get the best out of them.

Round 18: Forget about Being Liked—Respect Is Better

LESSON 1: Focus on the work and getting the most productivity out of your team. Do not try to be liked by everyone.

LESSON 2: Do not waste your time being angry at your boss. It serves little purpose. Use that energy to figure out how to get what you want and advance your career.

Round 19: Do You See Yourself as an Empire Builder? Should You?

LESSON 1: Building an empire is not the best way to the top; as a matter of fact, it may hinder your progress.

LESSON 2: It is OK to say no. If you are working nonstop, have no personal life, and are struggling to keep your head above water and the boss asks you to do more, just say no.

LESSON 3: It is OK to transfer some of your divisions to others. Get noticed by excelling at the work you keep.

Round 20: Are You a Martyr?

LESSON 1: Assess yourself. Do you fit the description of a martyr?

LESSON 2: Invest in your team.

LESSON 3: Do not assume that you are indispensable. No one is indispensable.

Round 21: Do You Have Impostor Syndrome?
Never Underestimate Yourself

LESSON 1: Corporate streetfighters do not have impostor syndrome!

LESSON 2: Wake up and give yourself the credit you deserve.

Round 22: I Have Good, New Ideas—But No One Is Listening

LESSON 1: If you have an idea, speak up.

LESSON 2: Exceptional ideas are rare. When your ideas are not considered worthy of pursuing, you need to learn why for personal growth.

LESSON 3: Implementation of your idea is extremely important. Coming up with ideas is an important skill, but it is essential that those ideas can be implemented at a reasonable cost and in a reasonable timeline.

Round 23: Be Decisive without Fear of Failure or Criticism

LESSON 1: We all make mistakes. Fear of making mistakes in your work life or personal life just leads to not trying the things that could change your life.

LESSON 2: Criticizing someone else is easy, coming up with ideas and strategies is hard. Don't let the critics discourage you.

LESSON 3: There is no room for blame. It is all about negativity. It makes the person who was blamed and those around them fearful and less likely to make contributions to the business.

LESSON 4: Failure is a part of work and life, and you need to learn from your failures. If you learn from your failures, they become more like lessons and less like failures.

Round 24: Are You a Leader, Follower, or Manager?

LESSON 1: Assess your abilities to decide whether you are a leader, a follower, or a manager.

LESSON 2: Contemplate your future career goals. If your personality and skill set do not match your aspirations, coaching can help open your eyes to where you need to change.

LESSON 3: No matter what category you are in, always work to be the best version of yourself.

Round 25: No Guts, No Glory—Taking Success to the Next Level

LESSON 1: Risks need to be taken to blaze a new trail and achieve greater success.

LESSON 2: Know your own appetite for risk and act appropriately, but if you are risk averse, do not blame others if you do not achieve what you had hoped for.

Round 26: International Business Is All about Culture

LESSON 1: Understand the culture of the offices and people you work with.

LESSON 2: Apply your cultural learnings to your management style.

FINAL THOUGHTS

In order to give you insight into how to handle the many issues you'll run into in the corporate world, I've taken you on my personal journey and given you a chance to see some of the key events and conversations that have shaped my career. Reading these situations will probably bring to mind things that happened in your own life and that you've seen around you and can relate to and open your mind to *other ways to approach problems* when they occur.

After I lost a job that I had put my heart and soul into, my eldest daughter, knowing my passion for chess, sent me the following quote:

After the game, the king and the pawn go into the same box.

—ITALIAN PROVERB

This is so true. At the end of the day, hopefully, we all go home to family and loved ones to have our real life. Make sure you have a life. Do not miss important moments with your significant other or your children in order to have more meetings or spend more time at the office. Go to dinners, ball games, and dance recitals and spend time with your family. I guarantee you that, as you look back at your life, you won't remember the meetings, but you will remember the times you enjoyed with your family. Your family, however, will remember all the times you did not show up because you put your work before them. There is life after work!

I know there are some people out there who will interpret this proverb as meaning that both kings and pawns end up in a pine box after death, but I choose to interpret it in a more positive sense. In chess there is always another game to be played and another chance to win.

Ultimately, you should be the hero of your own story. And that means that you need to take control and fight for what you want in life. If you are a *Star Wars* fan, you need to be Luke Skywalker. For my part I would be Yoda, teaching you how to make the best of the situation you are in. If you are lucky, your boss is Obi-Wan Kenobi, and if you are unlucky, your boss is Darth Vader. But now that you have read *Corporate Streetfighter* and put these strategies into action, you should be able to excel under Obi-Wan or handle Darth with success!

So are you now ready to put your new skills into play? It is time for you to show your corporate street fighting chops! And remember that clever strategy will *always* serve you better than confrontation.

The supreme art of war is to subdue the enemy without fighting.

—SUN TZU

ABOUT THE AUTHOR

Dr. Jeffrey Litwin is a seasoned corporate streetfighter, having served as CEO of eResearch Technology (now Clario) and MedAvante-Pro-Phase, as well as COO of WIRB-Copernicus Group. He is also the cofounder of Patient Genesis, which he sold to the WIRB-Copernicus Group. In those roles he participated in the acquisition of over twenty-five companies. Today he is president of Litwin Consulting, LLC, an executive coaching and strategic advisory firm.

Focusing on the bottom-line impact that culture has on business, Dr. Litwin has played an instrumental role in the sale of several multi-billion-dollar companies with offices across the United States, Europe, and Asia. Capitalizing on his passion for mentoring high-potential individuals and management teams to help them increase teamwork, productivity, profitability, and personal prosperity, Dr. Litwin wrote *Corporate Streetfighter*, published with Forbes Books in 2022. In it he shares the insights and wisdom won throughout his thirty-five-plus-year career, spanning a journey that saw him start as a physician who knew little about business and concluded with his transition into a successful business executive teaching the next generation of leaders what it takes to win by managing up.

ACKNOWLEDGMENTS

I want to thank …

My family for going on this journey with me.

My friend Russ for his invaluable advice on how to write a book.

My mentoring and difficult bosses for providing a lot of the content of this book.

My peers and coworkers who both celebrated and suffered with me over the past thirty-five years.

My team at Forbes Books for believing in the book and their editorial and publishing guidance.

Printed in the USA
CPSIA information can be obtained
at www.ICGtesting.com
LVHW091533080824
787695LV00002B/307